G000080711

THE GREAT LIE

Other Titles from the Author

In Divine Company

Theological English

The Trinity, Language, and Human Behavior

The Speaking Trinity & His Worded World

Finding God in the Ordinary

Struck Down but Not Destroyed

Still, Silent, and Strong

Finding Hope in Hard Things

God of Words

Christmas Glory

The Book of Giving

I Am a Human

THE GREAT LIE

What All of Hell Wants You To Keep Believing

PIERCE TAYLOR HIBBS

Copyright © 2022 Pierce Taylor Hibbs. All rights reserved. Except for brief quotations in critical publications or reviews, no part of this book may be reproduced in any manner without prior written permission from the author. For more information, visit piercetaylorhibbs.com.

Paperback ISBN: 979-8-9861067-0-0
Hardback ISBN: 979-8-9861067-1-7

Scripture quotations are from the ESV® Bible (The Holy Bible, English Standard Version®), copyright © 2001 by Crossway, a publishing ministry of Good News Publishers. Used by permission. All rights reserved.

CONTENTS

I
An Allegory for Humanity

———————

Along time ago, a man and a woman lived in a great house and tended a great garden. They rose just before the sun came up each morning. As the light gilded the garden, painting the green with gold, they worked with joy. They pressed their hands into the dark, damp earth. They selected and sowed seeds, tamped and watered sprouts, and the prints of their fingers were marked with holy soil. All day they tended to the plants, spreading growth by the soul in their skin. After the sun had set, they would sleep under pure, burning stars, and rise again to a new day.

They loved to tend the plants, but not just for the work itself. They loved doing it because someone tended *with* them. They called him "the Great One." They could not see him much of the time, though they had inklings that he was always just behind them, beneath them, beside them. They could always hear him, not in a common tongue, but in a language of adoration, love, and beauty, a whistling in the wind. They knew he was always present, always sounding himself to them. Everything they saw, smelled, touched, tasted, heard, spoke, and thought seemed to call their attention to the Great One rushing through the atmosphere, this loving and mysterious helper, their garden king. They were everywhere assured of and fulfilled by his company. So they woke each morning eager to work with him. They ran into the fields, calling his name, and listening for the whistle in the wind.

But one day, things changed. A black mist entered the great garden and began whispering in the same wind. They could not make out his words at first, but then the woman heard a sound clearly when she was off by herself. "Steal." They did not know what this sound meant, so they continued to work and rest as usual. But unrest was growing heavy in them, like a stone in their chest.

When the woman was by herself again, tending to the most beautiful tree in the garden—with silver bark and broad, heart-shaped leaves—the black mist whispered again: "Alone." She didn't know the meaning of that word either . . . until that very moment. Even then, she didn't *know* it, but she could *feel* it. It felt like an absence, as if the Great One were not behind her anymore, not drifting all around her. In that moment, nothing, not even the tree of beauty, drew her adoration and joy. Instead, the garden seemed mute and cold. And it was *there*—when the woman stopped believing in the presence of the Great One, that the garden began to disappear, tree by tree and plant by plant, along with the great house. All faded into the atmosphere.

She and the man awoke to find themselves in another place, a green country they had never been in before—beautiful still, but foreign. Yet they were most discomforted by one thing: they strained to hear voicings of the Great One in the wind; it took great effort and patience to make out any whistlings from him. And so they often believed in that little word they once felt from the black mist: *alone*. Their children and their childrens' children believed the same. Generation upon generation grew up in this new land nearly deaf to the voicings of the Great One.

But the Great One was not gone. In fact, he was still all around them, ever before their blinded eyes, ever within their ear canals clogged with distraction. They were deceived by the black mist, though even that seemed like a dream to them now. Had they ever really been anywhere other than where they were right now? Hadn't the world always been this quiet?

This is how the great lie was born, the lie that the Great One was not there, when he was truly everywhere, even in the presence of the man and woman when they believed it was only the two of them, standing before the tree of beauty. It was the lie of *alone*.

We are still believing the lie.

2
GOD'S PRESENCE THROUGH SPEECH

You and I are in a predicament, aren't we? We can't sense God physically, and we have trouble sensing him spiritually, so we *feel* as if God isn't here. As I write this, I'm sitting in my kitchen at the counter. I can hear the hum of the refrigerator. I can see the amber, illuminated wires in our hanging lights, just above the breakfast bar. I can smell the dull air that hangs in the quiet room—pine wood and the ghost of old bread. My left elbow and forearm feel the cool marble of the dark countertop. I taste the bitterness of black coffee.

Not one of these senses gives me direct awareness of God. My senses tell me I am *alone*. The great lie, introduced in the allegory, centers on that phenomenon, the *feeling* that God is not omnipresent, that he is not with me everywhere I go.

Now, if you and I believe that lie—and we all fall into unholy belief at times—there's no telling what we might do. For our ancient ancestors, Adam and Eve, the great lie encouraged them to disobey the God who loved them—the Great One. In one monumental act of rebellious confusion, Adam and Eve took what he said not to take in order to become what they could never be.

Think about Eve's situation for a moment. If God were physically present when Eve was tempted—if he were sitting right in front of her in a tangible form, as an old man—would she have eaten the forbidden fruit?

I know, I'm speculating. But in this case I believe speculation is biblically permissible and beneficial. There's no mention of God when Eve is confronted by the serpent in Genesis 3. Readers could easily but wrongly infer that God is somewhere else, letting Adam and Eve live on their own for a bit. But he wasn't somewhere else. He *couldn't* be somewhere else. He was right there; he was present, because he's *always* present.

How was he present? That's a question with great gravity. In fact, if we have no answer to that question, we're in a world of trouble, and we may not even know it. If you're reading this right now and don't have an answer, you may be having a hard time believing in God's presence in your own life. You may be functionally living as if God were *not* omnipresent. And to live that way is a lie, *the great lie*, and all of hell is bent on your continual belief in it. If Satan and his marauding minions can get you to believe that God isn't really present, they've won half the battle. The rest of that battle focuses on you *acting* in light of that lie.

We're going to delve into some theology in this book. It may seem abstract at times, but I don't want that to intimidate you. Nor do I want you to think that this is a book primarily about ideas. This is an immensely practical book, grounded in realities that you live through each day. But to get to the practical applications, we need to wade through some theological thickets. As we wade, I promise we'll end up with applications that can dramatically change your spiritual life. You may even see changes today, if you're looking for them.

The truth I want to introduce in this chapter will sound very abstract, but if you can open yourself to it, I think it'll change your perspective on God's presence. It will give you a sliver of light to follow out of the dark room of disbelief—disbelief that God is present, that he sees and cares for you in this very moment, that his love and faithfulness are following you around everywhere you go, more graciously and mercifully loyal than any golden retriever. God is always in the room.

Now, let's get to it. It's time to re-envision the presence of God so we can assault the great lie wherever and whenever it confronts us.

Spoken Presence

In this book, we're going to speak together. I was going to say I'm about to "argue" for something, but we don't have to be that formal. We're talking, you and I, and it's a talk that's going to have implications. In fact, the reason I'm presenting this whole book as a conversation is that God, in a way, presents his presence to us *as* a conversation and *in* a conversation.

So, here's how I'm going to start the conversation: *God is always present with us through his speech.* He's present in other ways as well, but I'm focusing on this truth with you in the following pages. We're going to unpack it, but let me explain why I'm starting this way.

First, this is what the Bible teaches, and I believe the Bible is God's word, wholly true and trustworthy.

Second, God is a Spirit (John 4:24), and so the typical

criteria we use to judge whether or not someone is present (i.e., our physical senses) don't usually apply.[1]

Third, while this conversation starter might seem like a letdown for people excited about a practical book, it's actually very encouraging. Our physical senses are limited in what they can perceive. Having God present through his speech means that such limitations melt away. We can *know* that God is present everywhere even though we might not *sense* him. Our knowledge of the truth glides on thermals far above the senses. That's good news, even if it's initially frustrating. Let me say it one more time, because this gets lost on us. *It's good news that God is an invisible Spirit and is present with us through his speech.*

We can know *that God is present everywhere even though we might not* sense *him.*

Now, in order to get at how God is present through his speech, we have to know something about the nature of God. As I've written elsewhere, God is a speaking God.[2] He speaks to

---

1. I say "usually" because Scripture reveals theophanies of God, where he presents himself in a physical form to his people. But these theophanies had a special place and purpose in the story of redemption. The final and ultimate theophany for us is the incarnation, where God takes on human flesh and then dwells in us by his Holy Spirit through faith. For an introduction to theophany, see Vern Poythress's *Theophany: A Biblical Theology of God's Appearing* (Wheaton, IL: Crossway, 2018).

2. Pierce Taylor Hibbs, *The Speaking Trinity & His Worded World: Why Language Is at the Center of Everything* (Eugene, OR: Wipf & Stock, 2018). See also Vern S. Poythress, *In the Beginning Was the Word: Language—A God-Centered Approach* (Wheaton, IL: Crossway, 2009).

himself in three persons—Father, Son, and Holy Spirit. These divine persons speak to each other using what I call *communion behavior*—language. This language is of the highest order. It's a language of mutual love and glorification. The Father, Son, and Spirit naturally love and glorify one another without end. If this seems above your head, that's okay. It's above my head, too. I can state it, but I can't understand it. I can worship God for it, but I can't analyze it. It's okay for truth to be above us. In fact, that's where Christ is, and Christ is the truth (John 14:6).

Scripture also tells us that the Son is the Word of the Father (John 1:1)—easily my favorite metaphor of all time. Whenever the Father speaks, he speaks the Son in the power of the Holy Spirit. This should already be mind-blowing. How does God speak a person? How does he speak himself? I don't know. Again, truth is above us. It condescends to greet us, but it constantly draws us up higher, never content to leave us on the ground. As Aslan said to the children in *Chronicles of Narnia*, the truth is meant to lead us "further up and further in." In this case, the truth is that God's speech is utterly personal because the very content of God's eternal speech *is* a person—the person of the Son. When God speaks, he speaks himself to us, and when we receive his words, we receive *him*.

Remember Jesus's teaching to his disciples? "Whoever receives you receives me, and whoever receives me receives him who sent me" (Matt. 10:40). Receive the word of God, and you receive God himself. God lives in you through words. Words link you to Christ. Words link you to the Father. Words link you to the Spirit. Words are one of the primary means of receiving the presence of God.

So, when this speaking God uses words to utter all things into being (Gen. 1) and to sustain all things by "the word of his power" (Heb. 1:3), he's using a behavior derived from his very nature. God's eternal speech is the ground of his temporal speech. The intimately personal character of divine speech—its "Son-centeredness"—remains when God uses language to create, sustain, and govern the world we live in.

Have I gone too far into the theological ether already? Do you feel like we're staring at the sun? It's okay if you feel that way. I do, too. This is lofty stuff. But believe me, this is essential to grasp because it introduces how the invisible, impalpable Spirit of God deep down inside us is present with us. This is the life-changing truth of Scripture.

To make this more palatable, let me break down this spoken presence into two different types. If you have some theological background, these types correspond to *general* and *special* revelation.

Creation Speech

Let's call the first type creation speech. Not sure what this is? Look around you. The entire created world is a type of speech from God. In Romans 1, Paul tells us that God has revealed himself in "the things that have been made" (Rom. 1:20). That's *everything*. Everything in the world reveals God, reveals something about his nature and dealings with us.[3] In this sense,

---

3. This was my focus in *Finding God in the Ordinary* (Eugene, OR: Wipf & Stock, 2018).

we might say that everything in the world "speaks" of God. Nature is a sort of word from God. Jonathan Edwards wrote, "As the system of nature, and the system of revelation, are both divine works, so both are in different senses a divine word. Both are the voice of God to intelligent creatures, a manifestation and declaration of himself to mankind."[4] Nature is not the same type of word to us as God's verbal revelation (which we'll get to next). And we should always be careful to set apart the primacy of God's verbal revelation for our knowledge and salvation. Still, that doesn't keep us from understanding the natural world as a sort of speech from God.

In short, because everything created has something to reveal about God, something to say about him, and because it is the very speech of God that made and sustains all things, we can say that God is present with us through his speech, the speech of creation.

The great lie is that God is not everywhere and always present in his world.

I'll be the first to admit this is tough to grasp. We're so prone to believing that the world is "just there." The world appears to be a neutral, rather impersonal place, doesn't it? We often

---

4. Jonathan Edwards, "The 'Miscellanies': Number 1340," in *Christian Apologetics Past and Present*, vol. 2, *From 1500*, ed. William Edgar and K. Scott Oliphint (Wheaton, IL: Crossway, 2011), 237.

feel alone. At least, we don't feel as if God is speaking to us everywhere, constantly revealing himself in the things that he's made. We don't feel a call to divine conversation simply by walking to the mailbox each day. But—*please* hear this—that is the great lie at work in our hearts. The great lie, delivered in ancient times by a slithering serpent and woven into the tapestry of human history, is that God is not everywhere and always present in his world. But he is. He *is*. We'll look at the biblical origins of this great lie in another chapter.

Pause with me to consider something about speech. *Speech requires relationship.* To hear the speech of another, we must have a sort of relationship with that person. This is obvious with humans, since our relationship is already established by our common nature. Right now, I can literally hear and see my three-year-old scribbling circles into a notebook ten feet away. We have a common nature; we both hold crayons with our fingers and press them into paper the same way. But it's not like that with God; we bear God's *image*, but we don't share his *nature*.

Take another example. When my wife says, "Good morning" to me, I don't have to work hard to trust that she's speaking to me. We have a deep relationship—not just of two humans who share a common nature, but as husband and wife. Nevertheless, there's a sense in which I must trust that she's speaking to me. When I talk with her on the phone, this becomes more prominent. I can't see her or touch her, but I can hear her voice, and so I trust, I believe, that she is really speaking to me. There's an element of trust, of faith, at the heart of language.

This applies to God's spoken presence on a deeper level. Because God is a Spirit, I can't see him or touch him. But he has given us spiritual ears (cf. Isa. 6:9–10) to hear what he says. He's given us ears to hear what he is saying about himself through the world around us (Rom. 1:20; Ps. 19:1–4). He's given us ears to hear his revelation. And if our spiritual ears are unstopped by the redeeming work of God's Son and the sanctifying work of the Spirit, then we're in the perfect position to trust that he's speaking to us, and thus that he's present with us. But our trust, our faith, is required. For we walk by faith, not by sight (2 Cor. 5:7). We won't accept God's presence apart from faith in him, faith in his words, faith in his spoken presence. And without faith in God's spoken presence, we're left with the great lie.

Interpreting the Speech of Creation

But how exactly do we hear God's voice in the world around us and take comfort in his spoken presence? Let me start by giving you a model and then a few simple examples to flesh it out.

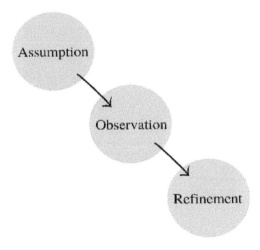

I've broken the model down into three steps: We start with an *assumption,* then move to *observation,* and then a *refinement* of our observation with Scripture. I should say, however, that my assumptions and observations are shaped by Scripture from the outset. Over time, yours will be as well, if they aren't already.

Start with a very important *assumption:* everything in the world reveals God. Everything—your mother's hair, the row of pine trees outside your window, the cotton shirt you're wearing. Everything. That truth is made abundantly clear in Romans 1:20, and it's reinforced by passages such as Psalm 19:1–4. We don't just *hope* God is revealed in something we see around us; we *know* he is. We have to start there. We grip that revealed truth with white-knuckled tenacity.

Now, make any observation you like. Really—anything at all. Take your dog, for instance. Here's our old dog, Buckley (may he rest in peace).[5] I observed him sleeping on the couch many afternoons, buried in pillows and wrapped in blankets like royalty. His sleep reveals something about the character of God. What, exactly? Sabbath rest? Peace? We need a biblical perspective, a microscope given by God himself that shows us more deeply what Buckley's sleep is pointing us to, so we move on to refinement.

For *refinement*, we ask, "What does Scripture tell us about sleep and rest?" Well, God was the first one who rested, modeling it for us (Gen. 2:1–2). And he sets apart a day of rest as holy. In fact, in Exodus 31:13, God says something quite profound (as he always does; he can't help himself). "You are to speak to the people of Israel and say, 'Above all you shall keep my Sabbaths, for this is a sign between me and you throughout your generations, that you may know that I, the LORD, sanctify you.'" Do you see the purpose for Sabbath rest? It's *sanctification*, our being made holy. Isn't that fascinating? Most of us only go as far as to say that rest is for our relaxation. The latter is certainly true, but why did *God* rest? Why does he call us to do the same? There's mystery here, and more than one answer. But we at least know that God didn't need to relax; he's all-powerful. And sure, maybe he was just modeling rest for us so that we'd see our God-given limits. But God is also utterly holy, and perhaps his rest at the end of creation is a portrait of that holiness, complete and content in itself. That would make some

---

5. Photo Credit: Tobias Hibbs Photography.

sense out of Exodus 31:13. We rest so that we may know that God sanctifies us, that the holy one is making us holy when we pause, when we stop, when we lay down. Rest, in other words, is a part of our being made more like God. When we stop, when our strivings cease, when we close our eyes, God doesn't stop working; he continues. Some of God's great work happens when your eyes are closed! Take a nap on that.

Let's go back to Buckley sleeping on the couch. Buckley isn't an image bearer of God, so he's not being sanctified in his sleep. (If he had been, I would've found fewer chewed up crayons underneath the dining room table.) However, his sleep is related to the rest that all animate creatures need in God's world. *His* need for sleep reminds me of *my* need for sleep. But my need for sleep also brings out my need for continual sanctification. Buckley sleeps to rest his tired frame; I sleep so that God might conform me to his name.

A daydreaming dog can serve to remind us of a Christ-conforming God.

So, Buckley sleeping on the couch is a sign pointing to the sanctification that results from rest—a holiness project for which God is wholly responsible. A daydreaming dog can serve to remind us of a Christ-conforming God who shapes and molds us even in our sleep to the image of his Son (Rom. 8:29). This is an example of *creation speech*. Something in the natural world revealed the character and work of God to me. God is present with me when I assume, observe, and refine because I'm doing all of that with his speech. God is present and speaks to me through the things that he's made. But I can't understand the things that he's made or what he might be communicating to me through them apart from his verbal revelation in Scripture.

How about one more example? Outside my window is a silver maple tree, whose main trunk splits into three as it climbs higher into the sky, reaching into the expanse like a prayer. A summer breeze is pushing the limbs back and forth. The papery leaves are turning on their stems and rubbing against one another. And as I look through the gaps in the foliage, I can see a strong blue sky. Is God speaking to me? It's taken me years to understand that the answer to that question is *always* yes.

The elements that I observe aren't "just there." Nothing in the world is. They've been spoken into existence by God and are upheld by divine language, by the word of God's power (Heb. 1:3). God has a purpose for that tree, and the purpose is both simple and profound: to reveal his nature and character. What is this tree revealing, specifically? Consider a few things. Again, note the stages of assumption, observation, and refinement, this time in a trinitarian context.

First, the trunk of the tree, as a strong and stable base, reflects the strength and stability of our heavenly Father, for in him there is no variation or change (James 1:17). At the creaturely level, that tree trunk has a characteristic derived from the God who spoke creation into being. I look at that maple tree and say, "Thank you, Father, that you are immovable. Thank you for always remaining the same when the winds of change keep blowing through my life." Is God *really* saying this to me, that he's strong and stable and immoveable? Is this really the content of his revelation through that tree? I have to trust him, to take him at his worded world, and measure the message I think I've received against the teaching of Scripture. I interpret *creation speech* through the *special speech* of Scripture. And when I do, I find it easier to acknowledge God's presence in the world around me. Remember that the world isn't mute; it pours forth speech (Ps. 19:1–4). Am I insane for claiming to have "heard" it, or is the rest of the unbelieving world insanely deceived by the great lie? The latter seems more likely, since the great lie would suggest that God's world is mute because God isn't present in it; he's not always and everywhere revealing himself through it. Scripture tells a different story.

Second, the summer breeze pushing the limbs back and forth, rubbing the paper leaves together, reflects the dynamism and movement of the Son of God. As the Word of the Father, the Son is God expressed, God in communicative action. The tree limbs and leaves move because they display a characteristic derived from God's Son. I look at the limbs and leaves and say, "Thank you, God, for always being active and engaging. Thank you for moving not just in the world, but in my soul." The movement of the tree is not at odds with the stability of the trunk. Rather, it is a distinct but essentially related part of the tree.[6]

Third, the gaps in the foliage revealing patches of blue sky

---

6. Note in my language here the gap between creation and the Creator. We can't say that a divine person is "part" of God, since God is simple and has no parts. This is an analogy, not an equation. And all analogies break down eventually, especially those regarding God.

reflect the context of the tree in its immediate environment. Analogously, the Holy Spirit is the context for the Father-Son relationship. The third member of the Trinity is the personal, loving context for the Father and the Son. So, there is context for the maple tree ultimately because there is context in the Trinity. The context of the tree is a display of a characteristic derived from God the Spirit. I look at the gaps in the foliage and say, "Thank you, God, for holding so much in harmonious relationship. Thank you for the great and deep context of the world, and for putting all things in the context of yourself (Acts 17:28).

As we already noted, this is related to the fact that God spoke and continues to sustain this tree, and every other one on the face of the earth. It's not just that God created things through his speech; it's that they continue to find their identity *in* that speech. As N. D. Wilson put it, "He's not merely calling [a tree] into existence, though His voice creates. His voice is its existence. That thing in your yard, that mangy apple or towering spruce, that thing is not the referent of His word. It is His word and its referent. If He were to stop talking, it wouldn't be there."[7] Mysterious, isn't it, that God's speech creates, defines, and sustains all things? That's the God-governed world we live in.

These reflections on my dog and the maple tree, examples of God's creation speech, might sound strange to you. Perhaps what I've said even sounds arbitrary. Can these things really

---

7. N. D. Wilson, *Notes from the Tilt-a-Whirl: Wide-Eyed Wonder in God's Spoken World* (Nashville, TN: Thomas Nelson, 2009), 43.

reflect God's spoken presence in the world? Am I guilty of perceiving merely what I want to perceive?

I answer these questions by returning to the earlier truths we uncovered in Scripture. If God spoke an ever-revealing world into existence, and if that world is, in a sense, always speaking about him (Rom. 1:20; Ps. 19), don't we *have* to say something about what God is revealing to us about himself in the world around us? Isn't that a biblical requirement?

God is always addressing you through the world.

The other option, as I see it, is to suggest that creation does *not* everywhere reveal the presence of God, that creation is mute when it comes to the God who made it. In other words, there are places in the world where God is not truly present *as the revealer,* as the one about whom the whole world must sing—rock, reed, and river. That, my friend, is the great lie, and I will *not* believe it. Don't believe it either. No matter what you feel, what you think, where your alleged reason takes you, don't give in. God is present all around you. He's always addressing you through the world. Even a silver maple tree can reveal profound things about the nature and workings of God. The three-personed Lord of creation is always right in front of us; our vision and hearing is just too poor to sense him. But the Spirit can help us grow stronger, to grasp by faith what we cannot hold by reason.

Let's recap the first type of God's spoken presence before we move on to the second. God has used speech to create and sustain the world (Gen. 1:1; Heb. 1:3). That speech is an analogue, an echo of the eternal Word of the Father. So, when God spoke and continues to sustain the world by that speech, there's a profound sense in which he is personally present through it, in the constant, sweeping atmosphere of Son-centered, Spirit-driven discourse.

Now, all of creation is God's worded world; that is, it everywhere reveals him (Rom. 1:20) and in that sense "speaks" about him. So, if we have the spiritual ears to hear it, we can interpret the speech of God in the world around us by using the model proposed earlier (assume, observe, refine). We need faith to do this, but God has always given this faith to his people through the work of the Spirit. This makes perfect sense, since all language-based relationships require a sort of faith or trust. If we reject this and live as if God is not everywhere present in the world he's made, then we're in the shadow of the great lie.

God's Special Speech

The second type of God's spoken presence is the most critical, since it's the only thing that leads to our salvation and our ability to interpret the first type of spoken presence. This is God's spoken presence in Scripture, what theologians call *special revelation*. I'm calling it God's *special speech*.

God is present in his verbal revelation to his people, the Bible. We've always needed this verbal revelation. We needed it even before sin entered the world. God verbally revealed himself to Adam and Eve in the garden, telling them what they needed to do. He told them to exercise dominion and stewardship, to multiply and rule over the world (Gen. 1:28–29). And in what theologians call *theophany*—God's physical manifestations among his people—God even appears to have walked and talked with Adam and Eve (Gen. 3:8).

This brings us back to the truth that God is present in his word, which is hard to comprehend but clear throughout Scripture. In Adam McHugh's language,

> When we speak a word it rushes out of our mouths and vanishes, but when God speaks a word his very presence is carried along with it. God is never separate from his word. God's word is saturated and penetrated by God himself—his being, power and wisdom—so much so that you get a word that is presence. It starts to make sense why the Gospel of John refers to Jesus, the eternal Son, as the Word of God. When you have words filled with the very being of God, you have a Word that *is* God.[8]

God is always present with his words, and he's given us his words in verbal revelation.

God's spoken presence in this verbal revelation underscores something profound but often overlooked: we're creatures built for *communion*, and that communion presents itself from the outset of our existence in the call of language—in its ability to bring us closer to each other. It's a call out of the self and into another, into *relationship*. For it's only through relationship

---

8. Adam McHugh, *The Listening Life: Embracing Attentiveness in a World of Distraction* (Downers Grove, IL: IVP, 2015), 94.

that we were meant to live. I love Geerhardus Vos on this point. He says that our being made in God's image means that we're always bent towards communion with him.[9] Elsewhere he writes, "To be a Christian is to live one's life not merely in obedience to God, nor merely in dependence on God, not even merely for the sake of God; it is to stand in conscious, reciprocal fellowship with God, to be identified with him in thought and purpose and work, to receive from him and give back to him in the ceaseless interplay of spiritual forces."[10] Do you see his focus on communion with God, on relationship?

> *Through language, God called us out of ourselves and into a relationship with him.*

Let me explain this a bit more. Our perception of and engagement with the world was designed to come out of our relationship with God, a relationship established through language, which I call *communion behavior*.[11] In our verbal interactions with the God who spoke first, we would come to see the purpose of creation (to glorify and reflect God) and our

9. Geerhardus Vos, *Anthropology*, vol. 2 of *Reformed Dogmatics*, ed. and trans. Richard B. Gaffin Jr. (Bellingham, WA: Lexham Press, 2014), 13.

10. Geerhardus Vos, "Hebrews, the Epistle of the Diatheke," in *Redemptive History and Biblical Interpretation: The Shorter Writings of Geerhardus Vos*, ed. Richard B. Gaffin (Phillipsburg: P&R Publishing, 1980), 186.

11. I develop this more fully in *The Speaking Trinity & His Worded World*, but you can also find a concise introduction to the idea here: http://piercetaylorhibbs.com/what-is-language-communion-behavior/.

place within it as image bearers. Through language, God called us out of ourselves and into a relationship with him. We were meant to do *everything* in the context of this spoken relationship. It was to be our vantage point for reality. But this vantage point, because of the great lie, would be forgotten in the fall, which is the topic of the next chapter. For now, it's enough to remember that our verbally established and maintained communion with God was (and still is) central to who we are.

But how was God present with us through this verbal communion? It's difficult for us to imagine because on this side of the fall, our communication can seem void of personal presence. But we must remind ourselves constantly of two biblical truths: (1) Sin has changed things, and (2) God's verbal communication is of a different quality than human verbal communication. We speak as *creatures*; God speaks as the *Creator*. What might this mean in the context of our current conversation?

Keeping in mind what we noted earlier about God's speech being Son-centered, we can say that when God speaks, there's a mysterious sense in which he speaks *himself*. This is very strange, but deeply *personal*. In eternity, the Father utters the eternal Word, the divine Son, in the hearing of the Spirit. We infer this from various passages in the Gospel of John (1:1; 16:13).

Now, we might naturally wonder what this means, and rightly so. We're heading back up into the theological ether, aren't we? What does it mean for God to speak *himself to himself*, for the Father to speak the Son in the hearing of the Spirit? We're at the borders of human understanding here, but we can at least say this: *God is a community unto himself.* He is, as Herman Bavinck once put it, not an impersonal monad—an impersonal essence—but a fountain of life and relationship.[12] God, in himself, *speaks.* I love how Douglas Kelly put it: "The fact that the eternal Son of the Father is called Word or *Logos,* seems to mean, among other things, that there is—and has been from all eternity—talk, sharing and communication in the innermost life of God. The true God is not silent; He talks."[13] God speaks not only to us, but to himself. Speech is part of who God *is,* not simply part of what he does. So, when we say that the Father speaks the Son in the hearing of the Spirit, we're saying that God speaks himself to himself in a community of love and glory. He is his own community. Thus, when it comes to God's presence, whenever God speaks (which is all the time, in the deeper sense), he is present with that speech, for that speech comes from God, through the Son.

Summary

I know, I know—this all sounds horribly abstract. We went from a lighter discussion about God's presence to what may seem like a rabbit hole on divine metaphysics.[14] But it's not a

---

12. Herman Bavinck, *Reformed Dogmatics,* vol. 2, *God and Creation,* ed. John Bolt, trans. John Vriend (Grand Rapids, MI: Baker Academic, 2004), 308–309; Ralph A. Smith, *Trinity and Reality: An Introduction to the Christian Faith* (Moscow, ID: Canon Press, 2004), 72.

13. Douglas Kelly, *Systematic Theology: Grounded in Holy Scripture and Understood in Light of the Church,* vol. 1, *The God Who Is: The Holy Trinity* (Ross-shire, Scotland: Mentor, 2008), 487.

14. If you're interested in more metaphysics from this perspective, I recommend Vern S. Poythress, *Redeeming Philosophy: A God-Centered Approach to the Big Questions*

rabbit hole, I promise. We're laying the groundwork here for our assault against the great lie.

I've summarized this before, but I'm doing it again here because it's so critical. We need to chisel it into the stone of our mind. When God speaks to create, govern, and sustain the world (Gen. 1; Heb. 1:3, Col. 1:17), that speech is an analogue, an image or echo, of his eternal speech, his eternal Son. There's a clear correlation between the speech God utters in Genesis and the speech that he simply is (John 1:1). The two are not identical; they're analogous. The words that God utters outside himself rely for their meaning and stability on God himself.[15] That means those words evoke God's personal presence. And because these words are always being "spoken," for God always governs and sustains all things through his speech, God is present *everywhere and all the time* through speech. That's God's *creation speech*, the first type of spoken presence we looked at.

Scripture is God's holy conversation with his people.

However, what's even more amazing is that, within a world that's filled with God's spoken presence, we're also personally addressed by God in his verbal revelation, in Scripture. Scripture is God's holy conversation with his people. Though complex

---

(Wheaton, IL: Crossway, 2014).

15. See Vern S. Poythress, "God and Language" in *Did God Really Say? Affirming the Truthfulness and Trustworthiness of Scripture*, ed. David B. Garner (Phillipsburg, NJ: P&R, 2012), 102–104.

and variegated, the Bible is one long conversation, one long act of communion, one long heart-felt message of fellowship, one embrace of reconciliation. And God is present with his words in Scripture as gracious and loving. You won't find that in the natural world. Herman Bavinck was clear on that: If you want grace and forgiveness, don't walk into the woods; walk into the word.[16] It's there that you will find Christ on every page, as God speaks to reconcile himself to us.[17]

In Scripture, we might appear to see merely human language. I see the same thing that you see: verbs and prepositions and nouns and adjectives. But that language is composed of words that rest upon the eternal Word for their meaning at every moment. They are words for our redemption, and they are the only words that stamp out a path to salvation with God at our side. So, once again, God is present through language—a spoken presence. And yet Scripture is much more than this.

Scripture: More Than Spoken Presence

Scripture isn't just the spoken presence of God; it's God's actual speech (2 Pet. 1:21; 2 Tim. 3:16). "The Bible is God's speech in written form."[18] We can't ever understate its brilliance. When we hold the Bible in our hands, we're holding the very speech of God! We're holding a holy conversation, a direct verbal

---

16. Herman Bavinck, *Prolegomena*, vol. 1 of *Reformed Dogmatics*, ed. John Bolt, trans. John Vriend (Grand Rapids, MI: Baker Academic, 2003), 312–314.

17. Peter A. Lillback, ed., *Seeing Christ in All of Scripture: Hermeneutics at Westminster Theological Seminary* (Glenside, PA: Westminster Seminary Press, 2016).

18. Vern S. Poythress, *Reading the Word of God in the Presence of God: A Handbook for Biblical Interpretation* (Wheaton, IL: Crossway, 2016), 27.

address from the God of our spinning solar system. Scripture is unparalleled; it's in its own category. And it's the only thing that can save us from the great lie that God isn't fully present with us.

Remember, we live in the country of the great lie, where we imagine the Great One is absent. Until God's Spirit revives us through hearing the word (Rom. 10:14), we're walking dead (Eph. 2:1); our spirits are fish out of water, longing for a God-atmosphere (which we live in and yet rebel against at the same time; cf. Acts 17:28).

It's equally true that, though spiritually dead, all people really do know God exists and is present. What are people doing as they possess that knowledge? They're *suppressing* it; they're pushing it down to the ocean-bed of their hearts.[19] Currents of the world roll over it, and life teems above it in feigned ignorance, but it's still there. It can't leave. It's the foundation.

> *We live in the lie. We need to be reborn in order to hear and see properly, in order to live in the truth.*

Paul says, "For the wrath of God is revealed from heaven against all ungodliness and unrighteousness of men, who by their unrighteousness suppress the truth. For what can be known about God is plain to them, because God has shown it

---

19. K. Scott Oliphint, *Covenantal Apologetics: Principles & Practice in Defense of Our Faith* (Wheaton, IL: Crossway, 2013), chap. 1.

to them. For his invisible attributes, namely, his eternal power and divine nature, have been clearly perceived, ever since the creation of the world, in the things that have been made. So they are without excuse" (Rom. 1:18–20). Deep down, on the ocean-bed of every human heart, people know that God exists and is present, but because of the great lie and our tacit belief in it, we suppress that truth. Until the Holy Spirit shatters that lie for us, as we come to faith in Jesus Christ and believe that God truly is speaking to us (in nature and in Scripture), we don't fully realize or appreciate God's presence. We live in the lie. We need to be reborn in order to hear and see properly, in order to live in the truth (John 3; John 14:6; 1 John 1:6).

Recall the encounter of Jesus and Nicodemus in John 3. Jesus told Nicodemus that he *must* be born again. He must be born by the power of the Spirit. He must enter into an entirely new perception of reality. In that new perception, Nicodemus would not only be able to identify Jesus as the Son of God; he would also begin to see the great lie fracture and dissolve. For it was Jesus himself who resounded the Old Testament truth of God's presence: "And behold, I am with you always" (Matt. 28:20; cf. Heb. 13:5). Jesus was God's presence incarnate, standing right in front of Nicodemus!

We'll talk more about Christ as the answer to the great lie in a later chapter. For now, we do well to note that our ability to perceive and live faithfully in God's presence is an act of God. And it has to be, since we're bent on suppressing the truth that God has revealed about himself. The shell of our suppression cracks against the granite of God's word, where we learn about the God who gave all of himself to be present with us forever.

What God's Spoken Presence Means

Our conversation has only just begun. While we could say more about God's spoken presence, we'll save that for the chapters ahead. Let's summarize where we've been in this chapter so that it's fresh in our minds for the next one. We'll need it fresh when we look at the great liar, Satan himself, and how the great lie was introduced.

Because God is a Spirit (John 4:24), we can't usually perceive or confirm his presence by ordinary means (the human senses). God's presence goes beyond our senses. His presence can be understood in various ways, but in this book we're looking at God's presence as a *spoken presence*.

What exactly does this mean? First, it means that we need to start by acknowledging the centrality of speech to God's identity. In God, speech *is* a person, the eternal Son, the Word of the Father, spoken *by* the Father *to* the Spirit (cf. John 16:13). God speaks himself to himself (remember that theological ether?), and this is simply part of who he is. John Frame has argued convincingly from Scripture that *speech* is an essential attribute of God.[20] It's not just what he does; it's who he is.

Second, it means that God is present in and through the world, with and in his people, through creation speech. I love how one author described our world: "The world cannot exist

---

20. John M. Frame, *Systematic Theology: An Introduction to Christian Belief* (Phillipsburg, NJ: P&R, 2013), 522–523.

apart from the voice of God. It is the voicings of God."[21] As the voicings of God, creation is saturated with God's presence, for the voice of the Father is the Son, the eternal Word, uttered in the breath of the Holy Spirit. God is thus present in the world because every fiber and fleck of it floats on the thermals of his breath.

Third, it means that God is present in a special way through Scripture, which is the very speech of God in written form. Whenever we read the Bible, we hear God's voice, and God is personally addressing us as we read. This personal address calls us out of the great lie and enables us to acknowledge God's presence all around us. Apart from this *special speech*, we lack the ability to perceive and properly interpret God's *creation speech*. Apart from the saving message of the gospel, infused in us by the Holy Spirit, we wander in the great lie.

Different Types of God's Presence

Before ending the chapter, we need to make an important distinction between what we might call God's *personal presence* and God's *omnipresence* (his presence everywhere). After all, there are scads of passages in Scripture that talk about God's presence as something that *is* with one person or group of people and is presumably *not* with another, or at least not in the same way (Gen. 3:8; 21:22; 39:2; Exod. 33:14–16; Deut. 4:7; 20:1; Josh. 1:9; Joel 3:21; Zech. 8:23; 2 Thess. 1:9). There are other passages that portray God's presence as a special

---

21. Wilson, *Notes from the Tilt-a-Whirl*, 98.

blessing (Pss. 16:11; 73:28). There are still others that locate God's presence in a geographic area (Eccles. 5:2), such as in the tabernacle and temple (Exod. 40:34; 2 Chr. 5:14; 7:1–2; Hab. 2:20). How are we to make sense of this? How can God be omnipresent, such as he's described in Psalm 139:7–12, and yet be with some people and not with others, or be in certain places and not in others?

The Dutch Reformed theologian Abraham Kuyper addressed this in his discussion of the Holy Spirit. He makes it an issue of *matter* vs. *spirit*.

> That which applies to matter does not therefore apply to spirit. God's omnipresence has reference to all space, but not to every spirit. Since God is omnipresent, it does not follow that He also dwells in the spirit of Satan. Hence it is clear that the Holy Spirit can be omnipresent without dwelling in every human soul; and that He can descend without changing place, and yet enter a soul hitherto unoccupied by Him; and that He was present among Israel and among the Gentiles, and yet manifested Himself among the former and not the latter.[22]

For Kuyper, God's omnipresence applies to the material world, while his spiritual presence moves in the spiritual realm. What Kuyper is calling God's "spiritual presence" is what I'm calling God's personal presence. When Kuyper speaks of

---

22. Abraham Kuyper, *The Work of the Holy Spirit*, trans. Henri De Vries (Chattanooga, TN: AMG, 1995), 128.

God's omnipresence in reference to matter, you can think of God's creation speech, his spoken presence with reference to all of creation. God's spiritual or personal presence is tied to his special speech.

Keep this distinction in mind throughout the book as we talk about God's presence. Whenever it's appropriate, I'll remind us of this so that we get a sense of how God is present with us and what that means for us practically.

Reflection Questions and Prayer

1. In what ways have you sensed God's presence in your own life?

2. When you don't sense God's presence, how does that make you feel? What sorts of decisions do you make? Think of a specific example.

3. Do you use God's *special speech* to help you understand *creation speech*? Offer an example.

4. How does God's *spoken presence* bring you comfort regarding the instability of your senses? In other words, why is it *good* news that God's presence is a spoken presence?

5. What are the implications of living *as if* God were not everywhere and always present?

Prayer

Lord of all-consuming presence,
Father, Son, and Spirit,

I know you speak,
But I don't hear it.
Your voice is all around me,
But my ears and eyes are blocked.
Help me to believe
That you are all around me,
That you are deep inside me,
That you have ridden words
Into my heart,
And now your home is *here*.
Help me to hear your voice in nature
As I hear your voice in Scripture.
Let your special revelation
Peel the scales from my eyes
So that I see your glory
In a world brimming with beauty.

3
THE FATHER OF LIES AND HIS GREAT LIE

C an we pause for a second? (This is a conversation, remember.) I want to be careful. I've said that this book is practical, and yet in the previous chapter we were drifting in and out of the theological ether, waxing on about a mysterious *spoken presence* of God. For some readers, that might have sounded like the *opposite* of practical. Wouldn't it be more practical to describe how we can *feel* God's presence?

We're dealing with the truth, and the truth is granite. We don't shape *it* to us; it shapes *us* to itself. The truth about God is that he's a Spirit. That doesn't mean we can't feel his presence in some emotional or spiritual sense. We certainly can. Many of us have experiences of grandeur or intimate consolation too great for description. We've tasted and seen that the Lord is good, very good. I'm not contesting any of that. What I'm contesting is the idea that God's presence works like any other person's physical presence. It doesn't. And that's good news. God's presence isn't restricted to the means we're accustomed to. It draws us into new vistas of faith and hope, new landscapes that stretch our vision beyond the tiny experiential frames we stare at. God's spoken presence is more constant, more powerful, more trustworthy than anything else. In fact, it's so immense and all-consuming that we have trouble perceiving it.

Think of it this way. What if an alien from a distant realm

in our cosmos approached you and said, "Hey, what's it like to thrive on oxygen?" I'm guessing you wouldn't jump to respond. Why? Because it's hard to imagine *not* thriving on oxygen. It's part of our life-giving atmosphere. We don't spend our thoughts analyzing our need for air; we just breathe it. All the time. It's a constant, pervasive reality for us. And because it's so pervasive, it's hard to explain. It's just fundamental to existence.

Deep, divine syllables—that's our environment.

That's what God's spoken presence is to creation. God spoke to create; God speaks to sustain and govern; God speaks to his creatures in nature; God speaks to his creatures in Scripture. Speech. Speech. Speech. Deep, divine syllables—that's our environment. Remember when Paul quoted Epimenides, the Cretan philosopher, claiming that truth for God? "In him we live and move and have our being" (Acts 17:28). In whom? In the God who is always speaking, in the God who speaks to himself, speaks to create, speaks to govern, speaks to reveal himself in nature, speaks to reveal himself verbally to his people. We live in God's spoken presence. It's so pervasive that we have trouble articulating it. And because sin has blinded our eyes and deafened our ears, we even have trouble remembering it. Forgetfulness dribbles into doubt, and doubt hardens into disbelief. Many of us act as if God is not really present. *That's the great lie.*

Even as I write these words, my head spins. The God who

breathes out the breakers each day and brings them back, whose words burgeon into trees that "bespeak a generosity of spirit,"[1] who calls caterpillars from wrapped sleep into rainbowed resurrection, who dug out a dynasty from a stone-slinging shepherd boy and was yet content to let our spit fall on the skin of his Son (Matt. 26:67)—he's always speaking, always present. Right now . . . where you are. Beneath and behind, before and beside. His words are holding your body together at this very moment. How could we ignore such a pervasive presence?

The short answer: by a great lie. That great lie is responsible for making you and me even think that God's spoken presence is an abstract idea. That's how potent the lie is. And we need to come to grips with that in this chapter by identifying who spoke it and how it was introduced. This is the lie, as the subtitle for this book puts it, that all of hell wants you to keep believing. If Satan can get you and me to believe that God isn't always present with us, he can get us to think, speak, and act in rebellion against the truth.

Satan's Identity and MO

Do you know who Satan is? In our day, that question might strike your ears as cultic. "Satan . . . like, as a real being, with a name and everything?" Yes. Our secularized culture says Satan is make-believe. At worst, he's an idea that gets in the way of our taking responsibility for poor decisions. At best, he's a nebulous,

---

1. Annie Dillard, *Pilgrim at Tinker Creek* (New York: HarperPerennial Modern Classics, 2013), 114.

invisible cloud that pre-modern thinkers attached a name to, but we know better now. In his incisive book *Live No Lies*, John Mark Comer notes, "people who believe in ancient ideas like the devil or, for that matter, Jesus himself are looked at with contempt and treated with the same intellectual incredulity as those who believe in trolls."[2] Be candid with yourself. Do you believe that Satan is real?

> *The best case scenario for a lord of evil is that the whole world would disbelieve in him.*

Get this: if you don't, he loves that; I mean, he *really* loves it. The best case scenario for a lord of evil is that the whole world would disbelieve in him. Then he could do whatever he wanted while people misdiagnosed the problems in their lives and ran circles around themselves. He could sit back and watch the whole world burn up in flames, smiling at the smoke. Come to think of it, that's exactly what he wants: complete destruction. But let me hit pause on that for the moment.

Jesus titled Satan without mincing words. And in doing that, he told us what Satan's *modus operandi* (MO) is, his consistent way of operating. But to grasp Jesus's title of Satan, we need to first talk about lies.

---

2. John Mark Comer, *Live No Lies: Recognize and Resist the Three Enemies That Sabotage Your Peace* (Colorado Springs, CO: Waterbrook, 2021), 14.

Lies

Lying is an ancient evil. It's the dark art of calling white black and black white. And it's one of the most dangerous behaviors because it doesn't often shout; it whispers. When you turn towards it, it's already too late.

A lie is essentially a false portrayal of reality. "Lies are unreality," in other words.[3] In Jonathan Swift's *Gulliver's Travels*, he calls a lie "a thing which was not."[4] That makes it seem as if lies are easy to spot. After all, who would really be stumped by someone calling black white and white black? It turns out that lies are a bit more complicated than that. The most potent lies lock arms with a particular truth and try to court it through a person's mind. If the courtship succeeds, it ends in marriage, and the person emerges legitimately confused about the way things truly are. Lies are less often blatant falsehoods (though there are plenty of those) and more often sly counterfeits.[5]

Another way to think of lies is to call them *mental maps*.[6] Lies take us places, just as truth does. We're always moving. We have to be. Just as some sharks will die if they don't constantly swim, moving oxygen-rich water over their gills, we

---

3. Comer, *Live No Lies*, 24.

4. Jonathan Swift, *Gulliver's Travels* (New York: Peebles Press International, 1975), 258.

5. On counterfeits, see Vern S. Poythress, *God-Centered Biblical Interpretation* (Phillipsburg, NJ: P&R, 1999), 167–175; *In the Beginning Was the Word: Language—A God-Centered Approach* (Wheaton, IL: Crossway, 2009), 219–227; *Truth, Theology, and Perspective: An Approach to Understanding Biblical Doctrine* (Wheaton, IL: Crossway, 2022), 87–88.

6. Comer takes this terminology from psychology and develops it in the context of our spiritual warfare. See *Live No Lies*, 24–28.

would die if we were utterly stagnant. We might feel stagnant sometimes, like a stick stuck in the mire, but we're not. We're always moving. And lies are mental maps of reality that tell us to move in the wrong direction. They give us a footpath that ends in self-centeredness. In *The Book of Giving*, I define love as self-giving.[7] And because the person who is truth (John 14:6) gave himself for us, we can say that lies bend us inwardly, towards self-taking. Lies are always in some way self-serving. What makes them tricky is that the mental map covers that up. It reworks the topography so that we think we're heading towards an attractive destination. But in reality, if we would peel away the top layer of the map, we'd see the true contour lines beneath. We'd see that the lie isn't leading us into a lush valley; it's leading us to a cliff edge.

So, one way to understand lies is to see them as *mental maps that lead us towards self-centeredness and death*. In contrast, truth is a mental map of reality that leads us towards self-giving and life. Jesus, who *is* the truth, gave himself and then received Spirit-infused life for eternity. Truth is self-giving that leads to life; lying is self-taking that leads to death. Is that contrast stark enough for you?

Jesus's Title for Satan

Now we're able to see the depth of Jesus's title for Satan. Are you ready? It's concise but chilling: *the father of lies*. That's his language in John 8:44. "He was a murderer from the beginning,

---

7. *The Book of Giving: How the God Who Gives Can Make Us Givers* (Independently published, 2021).

and does not stand in the truth because there is no truth in him. When he lies, he speaks out of his own character, for he is a liar and the father of lies." The word translated as "character" is very important. It's a word often translated in other contexts as "oneself." Jesus is saying that lying is part of Satan's *self*. It's an integral marker of who he is, not simply what he does occasionally. Jesus calls him the father of lies because every lie, every little act of deception the world has ever known, traces its dark lineage back to him. This marker of the devil's identity is utterly critical. The moment we forget *it* is the moment we forget *him*.

As the father of lies, at war with the person of truth (Jesus Christ), Satan has an identity that blends seamlessly into his strategy. What is that strategy? There are several ways we could explain this, but I've found Comer's portrayal (which traces back to the early church) clear and helpful.[8] Here it is in visual form

Deceptive Ideas

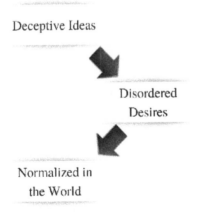

Disordered
Desires

Normalized in
the World

---

8. Comer, *Live No Lies*, 57–70.

Satan proclaims *lies* that play to *disordered desires* that are *normalized* in a fallen world. Simple enough? Lies, we saw, are deceiving mental maps that don't portray reality as it is, and they ultimately lead to death. "Disordered desires" means that we have certain desires that should be prioritized, and others that should be downplayed, and still others that should be battled. Satan's lies target desires that should either be lower on our priority list or absent altogether. Here's an example.

One of Satan's longest-standing lies is that *I* have priority. I should be thinking of *me* before I think of others. This "black" contrasts starkly with the "white" of God's commands throughout Scripture, especially Paul's words in Philippians 2:3, "Do nothing from selfish ambition or conceit, but in humility count others more significant than yourselves." I remember reading a book to my daughter years ago—for the *fourth* time that night. She asked for a fifth reading, and I said no. Why? Because I didn't want to read it again, and in that moment I believed the lie that life is about me, at least some of it. "I *deserve* a break from this, right? Shouldn't my reading preferences get an ounce of attention?" Satan's lie played to the disordered desire of my own reading preferences. But those preferences and the priority of self are normalized in our world. The world says, "Hey, you gave this kid four readings of a book with no coherence and a haphazard rhyme scheme. You deserve a break. Your daughter isn't the only person in the world who has value." Do you see how it works? Lies, disordered desires, and then normalization. In a matter of seconds, I made a toddler cry because I wasn't willing to give her another two minutes of my time. What an embarrassment!

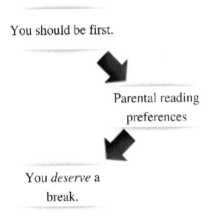

You should be first.

Parental reading
preferences

You *deserve* a
break.

Satan won that round. But I learned my lesson. Guilt can be an effective teacher. Everytime after that I made sure I reminded myself that bedtime reading isn't about *me*; it's about *them*. For those precious minutes, I front the truth that my kids are more significant than I am. I give them priority. That's not normalized in our world. But that's an encouragement to my faith. Jesus can never be normalized in a world constantly bent on itself.

This is a small-scale example of what happens all over the world, in every human's life, at every second of the day. This is Satan's MO: lies, disordered desires, normalization. It's a strategy so simple and so easily employed that we're able to pass it off as a character flaw on our part. "Whoops. I made the wrong decision." True as that may be, you weren't the only one involved. Lies are pervasive, especially the great lie. Think about it: Could I have treated my daughter that way if I truly believed that God was sitting on the opposite side of the room in the other bed? I don't think so. The great lie was behind the more subtle lies drifting through my head. This is the way it is in our world. Truth and deception are as pervasive as air molecules. Lies are drifting around you right now. At this very moment. But so is the truth. The tragedy is that we're mostly ignorant of all this.

In the remainder of this chapter, we'll look at how the great lie took shape in the Garden of Eden, since that's what led to all of the lesser lies we see in our world. This is going to set us up to understand how Satan and his host still aim to spread the great lie around every corner of creation, including your life and mine. In the following chapter, we'll see the great lie at work in Job 1–2 and Matthew 4.

Attacking God's Character

Brace yourself for some more theology. Because God is God and we are not, there's something we have to understand at the outset of Genesis 3. Bear with me as we enter into the theological ether again.

God is *one*. Recall the prayer known as the *shema*: "Hear, O Israel: The Lord our God, the Lord is one" (Deut. 6:4). Though God is *three* persons, he is *one* essence.[9] In relation to this,

---

9. For an introduction to the doctrine of the Trinity, I recommend Robert Letham, *The Holy Trinity: In Scripture, History, Theology, and Worship*, rev. and exp. ed.

theologians also talk about God's *simplicity*. He cannot be torn into parts. Herman Bavinck calls this God's "inner qualitative oneness."[10] What in the world does that mean? Well, it means that we can't break God down into parts or separate *who he is* from *what he's like*.[11] Whenever and wherever God is, we get *all* of him. When he acts in a certain way in history, one of his attributes (e.g., justice, mercy, grace, power) may be prominent, but all of the other attributes are there as well. God is always *wholly* God. When he enacts justice, he's still loving, patient, kind, long-suffering, beautiful, etc.

Another way to express this truth is to say that all of God's attributes are perspectives on each other; they're all interrelated.[12] I've quoted Geerhardus Vos before, and I've found him to be insightful here: "We may be content to say that all God's attributes are related most closely to each other and penetrate each other in the most intimate unity."[13] Because of God's unity, each attribute of God can serve as a perspective

---

(Phillipsburg, NJ: P&R, 2019).

10. Herman Bavinck, *God and Creation*, vol. 2 of *Reformed Theology*, ed. John Bolt, trans. John Vriend (Grand Rapids, MI: Baker Academic, 2004), 170.

11. See Vern S. Poythress, *The Mystery of the Trinity: A Trinitarian Approach to the Attributes of God* (Phillipsburg, NJ: P&R, 2020), 69–76.

12. Bavinck: "God is so abundantly rich that we can gain some idea of his richness only by the availability of many names. Every name refers to the same full divine being, but each time from a particular angle, the angle from which it reveals itself to us in his works. God is therefore simple in his multiplicity and manifold in his simplicity (Augustine)." *God and Creation*, 177.

13. Geerhardus Vos, *Theology Proper*, vol. 1 of *Reformed Dogmatics*, ed. and trans. Richard B. Gaffin, Jr. (Bellingham, WA: Lexham, 2012), the section entitled "Names, Being, and Attributes of God."

on all the others.[14] Put differently, "each attribute describes the whole of God, not just a part of him. If so, it also describes every other attribute, because all the attributes belong to who God is."[15]

Why am I saying all this, and what does it have to do with Satan as the father of lies? We need to grasp what happens when someone attacks the character of God as Satan did in Genesis 3. Because God is simple, when *one* of his attributes is attacked, there's a sense in which *all* of his attributes are attacked. When God's *authority* is challenged, for example, so is the *love, glory, holiness*, and *beauty* through which that authority is expressed. And so is the *presence* of God, which grounds God's authority and control. God couldn't be fully authoritative if he wasn't fully present. There is a sense, in other words, in which an attack on one of God's attributes is an attack on all of them.

Attacking God's Presence

Now, it's basically unanimous among theologians throughout history that what happened in Genesis 3 was an attack on God's verbal authority. Satan challenged the truthfulness of God in his word ("Did God really say . . . ?"), which was an attack on the authority of God, since God's words represent his authority. In fact, the eternal Word (the Son) *is* God, and the words God speaks to us as creatures derive their authority

---

14. Poythress, *The Mystery of the Trinity*, 545–554.

15. Vern S. Poythress, *Truth, Theology, and Perspective: An Approach to Understanding Biblical Doctrine* (Wheaton, IL: Crossway, 2022), 27.

from him.[16]

I've told my students in the past that "autonomy" (self-governance) is like a theological curse word when applied to creatures. Whenever creatures are said to pursue autonomy, we should gasp. There's only one autonomous being, and that's God. When creatures rebel against his authority, they try to claim autonomy; they act as if they can be self-sufficient, that they can go their own way. John Frame even goes as far as to say that autonomy lies at the heart of every sin.[17] Autonomy is what Satan encourages Adam and Eve to pursue, as we'll see momentarily. He tells Adam and Eve to go their own way, to be a law unto themselves. That is a direct attack on God's authority, since God is the only one who is autonomous. But based on what we just noted concerning God's oneness and simplicity, it's also a tacit attack on all of God's other attributes.

An attack on one of God's attributes is an attack on all of them.

In this book, we're focusing on God's presence. So we can keep our attention there for now. When Satan attacked God's authority by attacking his word, he also attacked God's presence. To dismiss God's authority is also to dismiss the presence of

---

16. See John Frame, *Systematic Theology: An Introduction to Christian Belief* (Phillipsburg, NJ: P&R, 2013), 522. This is also where Frame discusses speech as an essential divine attribute of God.

17. John M. Frame, *The Doctrine of the Word of God*, A Theology of Lordship (Phillipsburg, NJ: P&R, 2010), 17.

God that stands behind that authority. So, when Satan uttered the question, "Did God really say . . . ?" (Gen. 3:1), there's a sense in which he's also asking, "Is God really here to uphold his word?"[18]

You can also approach it from the opposite direction. If God isn't present, he can't be authoritative. Questioning his authority is thus questioning his presence. When we're talking about God, "Is God really here?" and "Did God really say?" are inseparable questions. The bottom line is that Satan wasn't just challenging God's authority in Genesis 3. He was also challenging God's *presence* (along with the rest of God's attributes). How did he do this, and what does it mean for us?

To Speak "As If"

I often tell my kids, "It's not just *what* you say; it's *how* you say it." The *manner* is just as important as the *matter*. I think this is where we get a sense of Satan's attack on God's presence.

We already noted that God is the God who speaks, the one who is a linguistic community unto himself. So it's not too surprising that an attack on God and his image bearers came through language.[19] However, I'm not going to focus as much on the serpent's misquotation and distortion of God's words

---

18. Note what Poythress writes about Satan's attack on God's presence in Genesis 3: "when we hear the voice of the serpent, into what sort of personal communion does that voice invite us? Who is this serpent, and what does he represent, and can he and his words really afford us an entrance into a presence that would displace and overpower and supersede the former presence of God?" *In the Beginning Was the Word: Language—A God-Centered Approach* (Wheaton, IL: Crossway, 2009), 107.

19. I develop this more fully in chapter 7 of *The Speaking Trinity & His Worded World*, "The Fall in Language."

in his conversation with Eve. That's important to examine and remember, but I want to focus elsewhere. I want to shift our attention to something more subtle and yet perhaps far more dangerous.

You see, before the cunning serpent twisted God's words and wielded them against the first humans, he introduced a *manner* of speaking. Stay with me here. I know this seems abstract, like our discussion of God's *spoken presence*, but this is where Satan is at his best. If we miss it, we'll find ourselves at our worst.

We all know that *how* something is said is just as important as *what* is said, if not more so. Let's take a moment and ask, "How did the serpent speak?" Here's the passage. What do you notice?

> Now the serpent was more crafty than any other beast of the field that the LORD God had made. He said to the woman, "Did God actually say, 'You shall not eat of any tree in the garden'?" 2 And the woman said to the serpent, "We may eat of the fruit of the trees in the garden, 3 but God said, 'You shall not eat of the fruit of the tree that is in the midst of the garden, neither shall you touch it, lest you die.'" 4 But the serpent said to the woman, "You will not surely die. 5 For God knows that when you eat of it your eyes will be opened, and you will be like God, knowing good and evil." (Gen. 3:1–5)

What's going on here? Several things! But look at just two of them.

First, there's a movement from distorting God's words, to adding to them, and then outrightly opposing them. Distortion, addition, then opposition. The serpent's words are bookends in this conversation. He moves swiftly from misquotation to defiance, using Eve's exaggeration as a stepping stone.

Second, we need to consider the dialogue between the serpent and Eve in the context of what God has already said. Genesis 2:17 leaves no room for ambiguity or misinterpretation—there's a single, clear consequence for going against the word of the Lord: judgment. That's what awaits anyone who goes against his command, who challenges his authority. Later in redemptive history, we see the pattern repeated over and over again: opposing God's word brings judgment (Num. 15:31; 1 Sam. 15:26; 1 Kgs. 13:26; 2 Kgs. 22:13; 2 Chr. 34:21; 36:16; Isa. 5:24; Jer. 19:15; 25:3–8; and many others).

Putting these two things together leads to a striking observation. Are you ready? This is the great lie. The conversation between the serpent and Eve is carried on without any indication that they truly believed in or expected God's judgment. Instead, they speak *as if* God is not present, *as if* they are separated from him (autonomy) and can act without fearing his wrath, which is grounded in God's presence. In fact, Eve and the serpent speak *as if* God is not omnipresent, as if he weren't there to carry out immediate judgment. At the very least, they disregard his authority to judge, which is still an attack on God's presence because we're *always* in the presence of the authoritative God.

Eve and the serpent speak as if *God is not omnipresent,* as if *he weren't there to carry out immediate judgment.*

In a discussion of what all men owe to God, Abraham Kuyper wrote, "Men owe God because He lives, exists, never departs, forever abides; and because from moment to moment they must transact business with Him."[20] We're always, from our inception to our end, transacting with God, engaging with him, living in relation to him. Elsewhere Kuyper writes, "Whether sinner or saint, angel in heaven or demon in hell, even plant or animal, each lives, moves, and exists in God."[21] You can see the tie to Acts 17:28. I love the way Lanier Burns put it in his book on God's presence: "Every life is a journey, and every person is formed by presences, for better or worse, the presence of God being the most important of all."[22] The bottom line is that we can't act *as if* God were not present because that's always a lie, the great lie. God is always present, and we're responsible to act *as if* that truth holds.

In Genesis 3, the great lie comes through in the *manner* of their speaking, in the *as if* behind their speech and actions. Satan and Eve keep speaking of God in the third person.[23]

---

20. Abraham Kuyper, *The Work of the Holy Spirit*, trans. Henri De Vries (Chattanooga, TN: AMG, 1995), 284.

21. Kuyper, *The Work of the Holy Spirit*, 609.

22. Lanier Burns, *The Nearness of God: His Presence with His People*, Explorations in Biblical Theology (Phillipsburg, NJ: P&R, 2009), 1.

23. Of course, this in itself isn't evidence that they're disregarding God's presence.

Satan doesn't acknowledge God's presence by saying, "God, did *you* really say . . . ?" And Eve doesn't claim, "God, *you* said . . ." God is being treated as a third-party outsider, as if there's a little sphere of communication among his creatures where he isn't present, where his word doesn't have authority, where judgment won't come.

That, I'm arguing, was the birth of the great lie, the lie that God is not always and everywhere present with us. The subtlety of the serpent is not just in his twisting of God's words. He's even more dangerous than that. It's in his *mannerism*, his speaking about God *as if* God were not authoritatively present.

I haven't read many theologians who point this out. Some might argue that this "isn't in the text." But I'd say it's definitely in the text, because all texts communicate both *matter* and *manner*, a *what* and a *how*. We usually focus on the *what*, but even when we do that, we assume a *how*. The same concept applies to biblical interpretation. When I read the verse, "I am the way, the truth, and the life," I use a certain intonation, and I emphasize particular words. I don't read it like a robot. I give it a *mannerism*, a *how*. We just don't typically talk about this. We're less comfortable and confident interpreting *how* a text means than we are interpreting *what* a text means. But we can't do one without the other. The *what* is always tied with the *how*. We can't emphasize one and ignore the other. We can't claim to say we've interpreted Satan's speech in Genesis 3 if we haven't commented on how he's speaking.

But it complements the rebellion they're committing against God's authority and judgment, which is a tacit attack on God's presence.

All *texts communicate both* matter *and* manner, *a* what *and a* how.

All I'm doing is deriving the *how* from the *what*, the mannerism from the context. I'm pulling out an attack on God's presence based on an attack on God's word, authority, and judgment.

"But that's not in the actual text," some people say. "The rebellion of the serpent, Adam, and Eve was behavior based on *words*, not mannerisms." I see the point, but words come from someplace deeper: the heart. Jesus himself said, "what comes out of the mouth proceeds from the heart, and this defiles a person. For out of the heart come evil thoughts, murder, adultery, sexual immorality, theft, false witness, slander" (Matt. 15:18–19). Evil thoughts, indeed. Could a rejection of God's kingly presence at the dawn of creation be conceived as anything other than an evil thought?

We have to go beneath the words, using the context to do it. Given the context of Satan's distortion of God's words and Eve's subsequent exaggeration, it's clear that both are acting *as if* judgment from God won't be immediate, that God won't do what he said he would (Gen. 2:17), that God isn't and won't be *present* to carry out his word.

The fact that we don't easily recognize this only compliments the serpent's cunning. This is a move by the father of lies, the origin of deception, the fountain of falsehood. Satan's cunning isn't only in his blatant changing of God's words. That's too easy. Growing up, I used to think, "Gee, the serpent wasn't *that* cunning. He obviously made changes to God's words and then flat-out lied to Eve." But now I see it differently: it wasn't just the *matter* of the serpent's speech; it was the *manner*. He spoke in a way that suggested God's absence. And his mannerism still haunts us.

If you're getting goosebumps, then you're catching on to what I'm saying. That was my original response to the idea: goosebumps. I mean, how often do we think about the manner of Satan's speech? How often do we think of the matter or content of his speech? You know the answer. Do you see the cunning? Do you see a mastermind of deception at work? How many hearts since Genesis 3 has Satan blinded simply by acting *as if* God isn't really present? Some might wonder, "What does acting *as if* God's not present look like?" It looks like a disregard for God's word, authority, and judgment.

"As If" and Rebellion

Once this great lie was born, the stage was set for rebellion. *Speaking* as if God weren't present led to *acting* as if God weren't present. Though we can't say for sure, Eve and Adam may very well have eaten from the forbidden tree because they gave in to the great lie that God was not omnipresent, since his word was not authoritative, and thus judgment would not follow. How could they have eaten the forbidden fruit if they truly believed in God's presence with them?

Again, slow down and process this. If God had physically appeared to Eve—in what theologians call a *theophany*—while she was still speaking to the serpent, would she have changed her response to the serpent's request?[24] Would she have eaten from the tree and given some to her husband? If the face of God were directly before her, how would that interaction have changed?

"But God *wasn't* present in front of Eve," you might say. That's true in one sense, but false in another. It's true that God wasn't physically present to Eve in a dramatic or majestic vision (theophany). And yet all of God's world *is* a sort of theophany, an appearing of God, because all of God's spoken creation reflects his nature and presence (Ps. 19:1–4; Rom. 1:20). "Created things reflect the God who made them. And through created things God shows who he is."[25] Just because God wasn't before Adam and Eve as a burning bush or a thunderous cloud doesn't mean he wasn't present. His presence isn't only theophanic. It's also a *spoken presence*, through creation and through his special verbal revelation—both of which Adam and Eve already had in the garden. In other words,

> Spectacular theophanies like Mount Sinai and the descent of fire at Mount Carmel stand out above 'routine' providences and 'routine' history. But theologically speaking, providence and history are never merely 'routine' but serve in a less spectacular way to display the same great truths about the power and greatness and kindness of God. Spectacular

---

24. For an introduction to theophany, see Vern S. Poythress, *Theophany: A Biblical Theology of God's Appearing* (Wheaton, IL: Crossway, 2016).

25. Poythress, *Theophany*, 85–86.

theophanies, therefore, can be seen as windows onto the realities about God that are always on display in providence.[26]

Always on display. In that garden, when Eve was addressed by a cunning serpent, God's presence was on display in the things that he made. He was present through his speech. And God's spoken presence is just as real as physical presence. The difference is a matter of *faith.* It takes *less* faith (and more awe) to believe in God's presence when a voice emerges from a burning bush. It takes *more* faith (and more obedience) to believe in God's presence when it's invisible, when it comes through the things he's spoken into motion. The latter is what our faith is striving for right now (2 Cor. 5:7).

In sum, before the entrance of sin in the world, both types of God's spoken presence surrounded Adam and Eve (creation speech and special speech). (1) God was present and revealed in the things that he had made, things that were created, sustained, and governed by his Word. (2) God spoke directly to Adam and Eve, as evidenced by Genesis 2:16–17. They knew that God was ever-present and good. Satan deceived them by speaking *as if* God were not, attacking not only God's authority and judgment, but also his presence. And since that moment, humanity has been plunged into the depths of doubt. We began our sad history of believing the Great One was no longer present.

Throughout the rest of this book, we're going to see just how pervasive the great lie has been in biblical history and in our

---

26. Poythress, *Theophany*, 91–92.

own daily lives, how it's made us ignorant of God's presence, and how God himself works in us to convince us of the Great Truth: that he is everywhere and always present with us.

Reflection Questions and Prayer

1. How does calling Satan "the father of lies" help you understand his attacks on your life, and how you might fight back?
2. Which of the three phases of Satan's strategy (lies, disordered desires, and normalization) do you find most difficult to cope with each day? Why?
3. Do you ever find yourself speaking *as if* God were not present? What's the result? Think of a specific example.
4. Satan's *manner* of speaking perhaps did as much harm as the *matter* of his speech. What are ways in your own life in which the manner of someone's speech does great harm?
5. Battling the great lie means embracing the spoken presence of God. Does that seem difficult to you? What do you think we can do as believers to encourage belief in the omnipresence of God and in his personal presence with us?

Prayer

God, we rebelled against your presence.
And we still do.
We believe the lie that you're absent,

And sometimes it feels that way to us.
But you are always there.
You're still there—*here*,
All around us.
Help me to trust in your spoken presence,
To know that your words bring *you* to me,
And there's no escaping your words.
When I sense Satan's lies about your presence,
Fill me with your Spirit and show me how to hope
In what I cannot see.

Reader Resource: The Presence Poem

I've written the poem below in an attempt to help myself remember God's omnipresence in light of Satan's lies. Perhaps it will help you as well. I recommend reciting it whenever you struggle to believe that God is all around you, and even inside you.

The Presence Poem

I cannot see nor can I feel
Everything I know is real.
God, your speech is here, with me.
There is no need for me to see.
I trust you here. I trust you there.
I trust you speaking everywhere.

4
SATAN AGAINST JOB AND JESUS

I am aware that what I talked about in the last chapter may come as a surprise to some. We don't typically think of Satan attacking God's *presence* in Genesis 3. We think of Satan attacking God's authority, attacking God's word, but not necessarily his presence. Am I just reading into the text what I want to see?

What I set out in terms of God's simplicity and his attributes has, I hope, convinced you that I'm not reading something into the text. It's *there*, because of who God is. A direct attack on one of God's attributes involves a tacit attack on all of them. And we have to take into account the *mannerism* of Satan's speech through the serpent, not just the *matter*. Given the context, it seems entirely appropriate to assume that Satan spoke *as if* God were not present. That would also fit with his MO as a deceiver. Satan's trademark is to portray reality deceitfully (his deceptive mental maps), to treat what *is* as if it were *not*. If the truth is that God is ever-present, then the lie would be that he isn't—that he's not present to uphold his word, that he's not present to judge. That's the *as if* Satan presented. That's the *as if* Eve and Adam acted on.

Still, before we look at the great lie in other areas of Scripture, it would help to look at two other passages where Satan is directly antagonizing God's people: first in the book of

Job and then in the Gospel of Matthew, where Satan attacks the Son of God himself. What do these passages have to show us about Satan attacking God's presence?

Job: Transaction vs. Relationship

The book of Job opens by giving us an insider's view on Satan's devilry. God allows Satan to attack Job . . . twice. Why does Satan want to attack him? Well, God identified Job as "a blameless and upright man, who fears God and turns away from evil" (Job 1:8). Satan scoffs at that remark because he's convinced God's relationship with Job is purely *transactional*. God takes care of Job, and so Job offers God worship and faithfulness. Note Satan's words in both attacks.

> [9] Then Satan answered the Lord and said, "Does Job fear God for no reason? [10] Have you not put a hedge around him and his house and all that he has, on every side? You have blessed the work of his hands, and his possessions have increased in the land. [11] But stretch out your hand and touch all that he has, and he will curse you to your face." Job 1:9–11

> [4] Then Satan answered the Lord and said, "Skin for skin! All that a man has he will give for his life. [5] But stretch out your hand and touch his bone and his flesh, and he will curse you to your face." Job 2:4–5

Satan accuses Job of being a transactional lover of God. And Satan takes two stabs at this. First, he says, "God, you bless Job materially, so of course he 'loves' you! You give, and then he gives. Everyone's happy. But watch what happens when you stop giving." When Job remains faithful after great loss, Satan takes his second stab. "God, you've given Job his health, so of course he 'loves' you! Everyone's still basically happy. You give your 'this' (health), and Job gives his 'that' (worship and faithfulness). It's just a transaction! But watch what happens when you take his health." In both cases, Satan accuses Job of going after a transaction rather than a relationship. The former is *quid pro quo*; the latter is rooted in self-giving love.

Satan accuses Job of going after a transaction rather than a relationship.

The rest of the book is about Job's friends revealing just how shallow their understanding of love is. They seem bent on upholding what I call "the deadly spiritual equation."[1] Really, this is just another way of supporting a transactional view of love. "If we do good, we benefit. If we do evil, we suffer." For Job's friends, he must have done something wrong to receive this suffering. He *must* have . . . because that's how the world works, like an equation, like a transaction. You give me "this," and I give you "that."

Now, here's what I want to point out in Satan's attacks. Satan says that Job isn't really after a *relationship* with God. But

---

1. "Job and the Deadly Spiritual Equation," http://piercetaylorhibbs.com/job-and-the-deadly-spiritual-equation/.

what does every relationship have at its center? *Presence.* Satan is saying that Job doesn't really want to be *with* God; he doesn't really want God's presence. For Satan, Job wants what God can offer, not God himself. Job's love of God's presence, leading to an authentic and loving relationship, is an illusion. For all intents and purposes, God might as well be absent from Job's life.

Just as in Genesis 3, Satan attacks God's words (his affirmation of Job's goodness and faithfulness), thus attacking God's authority. But he also attacks God's presence. Remember, a direct attack on one of God's attributes is a tacit attack on all of them. In Genesis 3, the serpent (representing Satan) speaks *as if* God were not present. In Job 1–2, Satan says God's presence doesn't really matter. In both cases, Satan's attacks run deeper than a mere opposition to God's word. An attack on God's word is an attack on all that God's word represents, including his presence, for God is always present with his words. In fact, all throughout Scripture, God acts through speech (think of God's *spoken presence* here). And as John Frame notes, "if God performs all his actions by powerful and authoritative speech, then his speech is never separated from his personal presence."[2] Satan's challenge to God's declaration about Job is also a challenge to God's real, relational *presence* with Job.

The great lie—that God isn't really present with his people, or that his presence has no relevance—is still going strong by the time of Job. What we see at the end of the book is how

---

2. John M. Frame, *The Doctrine of the Word of God*, A Theology of Lordship (Phillipsburg, NJ: P&R, 2010), 66.

God's authoritative presence completely overwhelms Job's comprehension. Job wasn't there when God formed the foundations of the earth (Job 38:4), when God was *present* in calling forth the currents in the sea and every earthly topography. For every blade of grass, every tensing fiber in earth and sky and sea, God was present. He's *always* present. All the great lie has ever done is suggest that he isn't, or that God's presence is irrelevant.

Jesus: With vs. Alone

When we get to the New Testament, we find Satan going head to head with the Son of God incarnate. This itself is already an attack on God's presence, since Jesus is the incarnate presence of God. Reflecting on the prologue of John's Gospel, where Jesus is referred to as the *Logos* of God, Lanier Burns writes,

> Logos is a name of God that identifies [God's] effective presence in creation, revelation, and salvation. The Word is the unique human person, who, as God in his gracious fullness, brings life to bear on a world that is dissolving itself in secular acids. . . . the incarnation as divine presence should be seen as an invasion of love (1 John 4:7–21).[3]

As the Logos in the flesh, Jesus is the embodied *presence* of God, calling us into a loving relationship with the Lord of all. This is critical to keep in mind when we read Matthew 4.

---

3. Lanier Burns, *The Nearness of God: His Presence with His People*, Explorations in Biblical Theology (Phillipsburg, NJ: P&R, 2009), 15, 21.

Is the great lie still apparent here, in Satan's three temptations of Christ? Yes, for all three temptations are attacks on the embodied *presence* of God. Whereas in Job the contrast was between *transaction* and *relationship*, in Matthew 4 the contrast is between living *with God* (in submission to his word, which bears his presence) and living *alone* (rejecting God's word and thus turning away from his presence).

The Spirit leads Jesus into the wilderness in Matthew 4, helping us see that this narrative is already set in the context of God's presence. Jesus didn't wander into the desert; he was led there *by the Spirit* (Matt. 4:1). God's personal presence was the road Jesus walked into the arena of temptation.

Whereas Satan attacked Job twice, he tempts the Son of God three times. Notice at this point the same pattern we found in Genesis 3. Satan goes after God's words, attacking God's authority, but this is simultaneously an attack on God's presence. Here are his three assaults on the Son of God.

> [3] And the tempter came and said to him, "If you are the Son of God, command these stones to become loaves of bread." [4] But he answered, "It is written, "'Man shall not live by bread alone, but by every word that comes from the mouth of God.'" [5] Then the devil took him to the holy city and set him on the pinnacle of the temple [6] and said to him, "If you are the Son of God, throw yourself down, for it is written, "'He will command his angels concerning you,' and "'On their hands they will bear you up, lest you strike your foot against a stone.'" [7] Jesus said to him, "Again it is written,

'You shall not put the Lord your God to the test.'" [8] Again, the devil took him to a very high mountain and showed him all the kingdoms of the world and their glory. [9] And he said to him, "All these I will give you, if you will fall down and worship me." [10] Then Jesus said to him, "Be gone, Satan! For it is written, "'You shall worship the Lord your God and him only shall you serve.'" [11] Then the devil left him, and behold, angels came and were ministering to him. Matt. 4:3–11

Three attacks on God's word, three jabs at God's authority, three dismissals of God's presence. In the first, Satan challenges God's previous declaration that Jesus is the Son of God (Matt. 3:17). He says, in essence, "Jesus, you don't need God to affirm your identity. Use your power to do that, and go it alone. Establish on your own who you are." Jesus rejects independence and clings to a relationship with the God who is always present. When Jesus quotes Deuteronomy 8:3, he's not just saying, "God's word is true!" He's also saying, "I choose a relationship *with* the God who speaks, not feigned independence *from* him."

In the second attack, Satan does the same. He challenges Jesus to go it alone, to act *outside* of a relationship with the ever-present and trustworthy God. Satan says, "Prove it to yourself that you're divine. Don't just trust God and your relationship with him!" Jesus responds beautifully: don't test a divine relationship. Putting God to the test would be the same as distrusting his word, which is bound up with distrusting his presence. Jesus chooses to rely on God's presence, to be *with* God rather than to go it alone.

In the third attack, Satan goes all out and asks Jesus to substitute God's presence for his own presence. "All these I will give you, if you will fall down and worship me." Worship is bound up with presence. We worship God because he is *here*. Yes, he's authoritative and gracious and beautiful and all-powerful—but he's here. How would we know about and rely on any of God's attributes apart from his *presence* with us? Our worship says, "Thank you for being here, for being *with* me." Satan asks Jesus to give him that worship, to exchange the presence of God for the presence of Satan.

In all three attacks, Jesus prioritizes God's word and trusts in God's presence. He doesn't believe the lie that any creature could ever go without it, or that it's practically irrelevant. God's presence is everything to Jesus. And that makes sense, since Jesus *is* God. God's presence is also a presence of personal *love*, which, again, makes sense, since God *is* love (1 John 4:8).

One writer describes this temptation scene as a war of "scripts," the guiding voices in our lives.[4] The true script Jesus had just received in Matthew 3 was beautifully pure and simple: *You are my Son, and I love you.* Do you see how that script is steeped in the relational presence of God? The false script that Satan keeps pushing is this: *You need to prove you're God's Son on your own, to show you're worthy of love.* The false script says to go it alone; the true script says to move in relationship, in a trustful acknowledgement of God's presence.

I'd like to say a lot more about this, but I'm saving it for a

---

4. Adam S. McHugh, *The Listening Life: Embracing Attentiveness in a World of Distraction* (Downers Grove, IL: IVP, 2015), 197–198.

later chapter, where we unpack the claim that Jesus is God's answer to the great lie.

Job, Jesus, and Us

In this chapter, we've seen how Satan propounded the great lie in the time of Job and in the time of Jesus. But what about us? I'm dedicating a few chapters to answer that question, but for now, let's start thinking about the great lie and the ways it may be affecting our lives.

In attacking Job, Satan accused him of being *transactional* rather than *relational*. In a transaction, there is simply an exchange. I give you *this*, and you give me *that*. Aside from the transaction, there's little to no interaction. Are we guilty of taking this approach to God today?

If we're candid, all of us can utter an embarrassing "yes." Each time difficulty or disaster strikes, we lift our eyes to the sky and say, "Why me? Why now?" Behind these little questions is often an expectation for reciprocation. "God, I gave you my life in faith, so why are you giving me *this*?" Do you see the transaction at play?

Jesus, as the embodied presence of God, gave love. We gave him enmity.

That transaction shatters at the feet of Jesus. Jesus deserved only glory and honor from God and from us, and yet he received ridicule, rebuke, rebellion, and ravenous hate, culminating in crucifixion. Jesus, as the embodied presence of God, gave love. We gave him enmity. If the spiritual equation was broken before the most holy person who ever lived, why would it stand up for us, whose lives are always riddled with sin and doubt? What happened to Jesus is a clear testimony that God is after something deeper from us. He doesn't want a transaction; he wants a relationship. And God is willing to forge that relationship at great cost to himself. He's willing to give us his presence even though we've lived as if that presence were a fiction. When Paul says in Romans, "while we were still sinners, Christ died for us" (Rom. 5:8), the import is this: while we were seeking self-serving transactions, Christ came to give himself for relationship. And relationships are formed and maintained through mutual self-giving.

Living with *God means listening* to *God, and listening* to *God means obeying him.*

In attacking Jesus, Satan told him to go it *alone* rather than to be content *with* God's abiding presence. Are we tempted to do this today? Choose your response: nod or blush. We know it's true. Much of our life is lived in submission to the world's call for personal independence, what we referred to earlier as *autonomy.* Pick up any secular piece of literature dealing with identity or self-expression, and you'll find independence praised as the highest virtue. This has led, among other things, to the great disease of loneliness. And perhaps that's always where the great lie brings us. "Mother Teresa called loneliness the leprosy of the Western world, maybe even more devastating than Calcutta poverty."[5] Loneliness comes from rejecting the divine presence we need to discern our value, purpose, and direction. The cure for this leprosy is the touch of God's presence (Matt. 8:3).

Jesus chooses a relationship with God by submitting to his Father's *word* and *will*. The Spirit gives us a new heart to do just that. Living *with* God means listening *to* God, and listening *to* God means obeying him. Adam McHugh wrote, "Listening is foundational to what it means to be human."[6] And since our humanity is fully restored only in Jesus Christ, the second and last Adam (1 Cor. 15:45–48; 2 Cor. 15:17–21), our humanity is tied to following of Jesus. McHugh calls this "biblical listening."

> Biblical listening is a whole-hearted, full-bodied listening that not only vibrates our eardrums but echoes in our souls and resonates out into our limbs. John's famous picture of Jesus as the Word of God means that Jesus's entire incarnated life, not only his parables and sermons, is the expression of God's mind. His life is God's speech to us. We are correspondingly asked to listen with our lives, and we are not truly listening unless we are responding to Jesus with all our heart, mind, soul and strength. This kind of listening is done on the move.[7]

---

5. McHugh, *The Listening Life*, 26.

6. McHugh, *The Listening Life*, 10.

7. McHugh, *The Listening Life*, 18.

Are we listening on the move? Are we listening in a way that concretely shapes us to the person of Jesus? Do we even know what that looks like? This sort of *life listening* isn't a fringe activity for Christians who appear to be doctrinally fit. Life listening is a matter of relationship. If we aren't doing it, there's a good chance our relationship with God is dwindling. If we want our souls to grow into the shape of Jesus Christ, we need to pay close attention to God's presence *so that we can be shaped to that presence*. Nothing else is more important than communing with God. And in that light, nothing is more critical than cultivating a listening life.

Reflection Questions and Prayer

1. What are your own reflections on Satan's temptation of Adam and Eve?
2. What are your own reflections on Satan's attacks on Job?
3. What are your own reflections on Satan's temptation of Jesus?
4. Why do you think Satan attacks the presence of God with his people?
5. What does Jesus's life, death, and resurrection reveal about the presence of God with us? How do you relate this to the Holy Spirit?

Prayer

God, Satan hates your presence.
He's always wanted to convince your people

That you aren't here

Or that your presence doesn't matter.

But I know you're here.

And your presence is everything to me.

Help me to follow your words

Back to your voice;

To trust your presence when I doubt you;

To interpret everything I see and think

In light of your being always in the room with me.

Reader Resource: Responses to God's Presence

How do people respond to God's presence? Thinking about this question can help us engage with each other, and it can serve as a testament to our faith. Below are several different responses that Scripture records. Do you know people who seem to respond to God's presence in these ways? When have you responded to God's presence in these ways? What motives do you think are behind the different responses? Try to support your answers with Scripture.

1. Open rebellion. "The Lord saw that the wickedness of man was great in the earth, and that every intention of the thoughts of his heart was only evil continually" (Gen. 6:5). There are people in the world who don't simply ignore God's presence; they actively oppose it. They tear apart loving relationships and seek to supplant them with master-slave governance. While God is relational, these people are narcissists, bent on self-elevation and dominance. In our own time, Vladimir Putin comes to mind. But there are much less severe cases that surround us in daily life.

2. *Distrust.* Twice Abraham distrusted God's presence to protect him, lying about his wife to save his own skin (Gen. 12:10–20; 20:1–13). His actions suggest that one of the moves people make when they distrust God is toward self-preserving deceit. They lie out of distrust, and they create a mess in the process, just as Abraham did. We'll look more at Abraham in the following chapter.

3. *Intermittent Awareness.* Many people are aware of God's presence in certain times and places but not in others. Jacob is a good example of this in Genesis 28:10–17. After waking from his dream, he said, "Surely the Lord is in this place, and I did not know it" (v. 16). Jacob became aware of God's presence when he wasn't before. God's presence, however, had been constant. This intermittent awareness can come to both those who follow God and those who oppose him.

4. *Spirit-led Acknowledgement.* Acknowledging God's presence is always a work of the Holy Spirit in a person's heart. This happened with Jacob in Genesis 28, but it also happened to Elisha's servant in 2 Kings 6. "Then Elisha prayed and said, 'O Lord, please open his eyes that he may see.' So the Lord opened the eyes of the young man, and he saw, and behold, the mountain was full of horses and chariots of fire all around Elisha" (v. 17). It was God who opened the servant's eyes to witness the presence of God in the form of his divine army. Acknowledging the truth of God's presence and then acting on it is a step beyond intermittent awareness.

5. *Spirit-led Reliance.* Acknowledging the presence of God is one thing, but relying on it is another. To rely on God's presence through the Spirit is to put all of your soul's weight on God, to set the anvil of your heart in his hands, to trust in him above all else. In 2 Corinthians 1:8–11, Paul expresses this sort of reliance. "Indeed, we felt that we had received the sentence of death. But that was to make us rely not on ourselves but on God who raises the dead" (v. 9). It was a work of God that helped Paul and his companions rely on God. They relied on God's presence with their whole being, pressed down by fatigue and death. People I've spoken with experience this sort of reliance on God's presence after major trauma, such as the death of a loved one or a terminal diagnosis.

5
A PATH OF REBELLION

N ow that we've seen the great lie hovering in the background of Satan's attacks in Genesis 3, Job 1–2, and Matthew 4, we can look at a few examples in other places of Scripture. These examples help us identify a path of rebellion against God's presence, a common acceptance of the great lie.[1]

In Genesis 3, the great lie fell like a stone on the glassy pond of humanity. The ripples lingered, and they're still with us. The great lie went from a hideous intrusion to a common assumption. Rather than being constantly aware of God's spoken presence, as Adam and Eve were before the fall, we're constantly deceived—always prone to believe that the ever-present God is absent from our lives, or, at best, is irrelevant.

The point of this chapter is not to be exhaustive, but to highlight a few of the other cases of when God's people gave in to the great lie. Think of these as representative examples. After this chapter, we'll turn a corner and start examining the effects of the great lie in us and around us. Then we'll look at the glorious solution in Jesus Christ as God's Spirit-filled response to the great lie.

---

1. For a fuller treatment of God's presence in redemptive history, see Lanier Burns, *The Nearness of God: His Presence with His People*, Explorations in Biblical Theology (Phillipsburg, NJ: P&R, 2009).

Cain

We've already seen the great lie at work in Genesis 3, but not long thereafter we meet it again in Adam's progeny. Cain, we know, killed his brother out of jealousy, spilling the first human blood, wetting the soil with a substance meant to stay on the inside. Could an act that atrocious be carried out by someone who believed God was present, who believed he was living before the face of an almighty Spirit?

The fullness of Cain's deception comes about when God asks him a question—just as God asked Adam and Eve a question after they sinned: "Where is your brother, Abel?" Cain responded like a fool, with a hint of sarcasm: "Am I my brother's keeper?" Chase Replogle reflects,

> How shifty was Cain's response? His returned question was an answer without offering one. He must have thought he was pretty clever. Dark and derisive, he scoffed at responsibility itself. His sarcasm gave away his juvenile contempt, not just for his brother Abel but for God. Our English word "sarcasm" tracks back to an old Greek word for tearing at flesh. Cain had spilled his brother's blood, and by his sarcasm, he clawed at the authority of God's question too.[2]

Yes, he clawed at the authority of God's question, but he also clawed at the authority of God's presence.

God wasn't actually asking Cain a question to obtain

---

2. Chase Replogle, *The 5 Masculine Instincts: A Guide to Becoming a Better Man* (Chicago: Moody, 2022), 43–44.

information, just as he wasn't actually asking Adam and Eve where they were in the garden.[3] When you're omniscient, you don't need to ask questions. God asks these questions to elicit responses from his creatures and to draw their sin out into the open. In response to Cain's question, God might well have said, "I know you're not his keeper; I am, and you killed him." The question precedes judgment. This is the same judgment grounded in God's presence in Genesis 3.

Cain's disregard for God's authoritative presence mirrors that of the serpent. As in Genesis 3, judgment was on the line. The great lie lives in the realm of *as if*. The serpent spoke *as if* God weren't present. Eve acted *as if* God's authoritative presence wouldn't bring immediate judgment. Cain acted *as if* God wasn't in the field with him and his brother, *as if* holy judgment wouldn't follow the first murder in history. And like Adam and Eve, he was dead wrong. Judgment came and overwhelmed him (Gen. 4:13–14). Why? Because the God who is *just* is also the God who is *present* to carry out the sentence. Rebellion against God's presence, introduced by Satan in the garden, continued to spread. Creatures were now stomping on a path of rebellion against divine presence, acting as if they weren't always living, moving, and breathing before the face of God (Acts 17:28).

Jacob

Sometimes rebellion against God's presence came in the form

---

3. On God's question to Adam and Eve after the fall, see "God's Great Gospel Question," http://piercetaylorhibbs.com/gods-great-gospel-question/.

of deeply-seated ignorance. In the reader resource from the previous chapter, I called this *intermittent awareness*. The story of Jacob's ladder is a clear example. Jacob fled from his brother and fell asleep in a field. After seeing a divine ladder reaching into the heavens, with angels ascending and descending, Jacob said, "Surely, the Lord was in this place, and I did not know it" (Gen. 28:16). The point isn't just that God was present at Bethel in a special way; certainly, he was! (Recall the distinction between God's omnipresence and his spiritual/personal presence.) The point is also that Jacob was *ignorant* of that presence. God was there in Bethel, but Jacob "did not know it." Why?

We would, at the very least, say that Jacob's ignorance was an effect of sin. But it isn't a far stretch to think that what happened with Jacob is related to the ancient suggestion of the serpent that we can live *as if* God were not present all around us. Remember that at this point in the biblical storyline, rebellion against God's presence is spreading. It had already swelled beyond comprehension after Cain, leading to the flood (Gen. 6:5–7). Now after the flood, the path of rebellion was being worn into the earth again. God's authoritative presence was not being recognized or respected.

Now, because of sin's effect on the world, I believe most of us would have responded to God's special presence in Bethel as Jacob did—not because of sin more generally, but because we've all been deceived. We all carry around within us a tacit belief in the great lie. We're all guilty of secret faith in something false, something tangible but temporary, like the stone under Jacob's head. God is *always* present, for the whole world is a testament to his divine nature (Rom. 1:20), but we're blinded by deception, often willfully. We don't see things as they truly are—partly because we're blinded, and partly because we blind ourselves. We *suppress* the truth (Rom. 1:18). We suppress it deeply.

> ## *We will not recognize and respond to God's presence around us if we lack faith and trust.*

In a previous chapter, I said that all speech requires an element of faith or trust. When it comes to God's spoken presence in the world, this is paramount. We will not recognize and respond to God's presence around us if we lack faith and trust. And yet having faith and trust isn't something we cultivate on our own, some spiritual garment we weave for ourselves with loom and shuttle. The faith and trust we need to respond to God's spoken presence in the world is something that God gives to those who ask him (Eph. 2:8–9). Faith is a gift we receive, not a garment we weave. It's God's offering, not our making.

What we learn from Jacob is that God's personal or spiritual presence might be right in front of us while we're busy trying to fall asleep on a stone. We need God's help to see and sense him.

Abraham

Seeing or sensing God's presence is one thing, but lying to

others out of distrust in God's presence is another. Abraham, a father of *faith* (Heb. 11:8–9), took another step on the path of rebellion against God's presence. He distrusted God's protective presence, turning to lies as an alternative solution. That shouldn't be so surprising: if the truth is that God's spoken presence fills the cosmos, the only other option we have is to believe in a lie, to think that God's presence is insufficient and that we need to take matters into our own hands. You can see the echo of Genesis 3 here.

Abraham was scared of losing his life when he went into another kingdom. And so he lied about his wife to save his own skin. He did this not once, but twice (Gen. 12:10–20; 20:1–13). Abraham's lie expresses many things, but chief among them is a distrust in the protective presence of God.

Whenever one of God's people enters a threatening situation, God's assurance is his presence.

We might not think of God's presence as *protective*, but whenever one of God's people enters a threatening situation, God's assurance is his presence: "I will be with you" or "I am with you" (Gen. 26:3; 28:15; 31:3; 48:21; Exod. 3:12; 4:12, 15; Deut. 31:6, 8, 23; Josh. 1:5; Judg. 6:16; 2 Sam. 7:9; 1 Chr. 17:8; 28:20; and many others). When Abraham enters a new kingdom with his beautiful wife, it's *God's presence* that's meant to protect him, especially as that presence was promised to him via covenant (Gen. 12:1–3). But Abraham distrusts that presence and lies, telling the people that Sarah is his sister. He lies in fear, assuming that the men of the region will kill him out of jealousy.

And look what happens in both cases: destruction ensues. In Egypt, plagues follow from Abraham's lie about his wife (Gen. 12:17). The lie might bring some protection for Abraham, but it brings destruction to others. People suffer needlessly because of Abraham's distrust. And like us, Abraham is a slow learner; he doesn't get the lesson the first time. In Egypt, there were plagues. In Abimelech's kingdom, there was a terrifying death-dream (Gen. 20:3). Nothing good comes from lies. Everything good comes from trusting in God's spoken presence.

When you think about it, Abraham's lie mirrors the great lie, doesn't it? The great lie says, "God isn't here. Or, if he is, that's irrelevant." Abraham's lie says, "God won't be here to protect me. Or, if he is here, it won't help." In both lies, God's authoritative presence is disregarded. In both cases, creatures fail to take God at his word. And in both cases, the implications are terrifying.

Elisha's Servant

Not all those who tread on the path of rebellion do so with direct willingness as Abraham did. Jacob was one example. Some tread on the path of rebellion simply because they've been influenced by a fallen world for so long, a world that fails to accept and submit to the authoritative spoken presence of God. Elisha's servant in 2 Kings is another representative example.

When Elisha's servant fears the Assyrian army, Elisha prays that his servant's eyes would be opened so that he could see a heavenly army so great it would make any man go weak at the knees (2 Kgs. 6:17–20). Elisha could see God's presence with them in the form of a divine army, but his servant couldn't. His servant was blinded somehow. For whatever reason, he could not sense the clear and powerful presence of God all around them.

Just imagine how this unfolded. A landscape that was barren and a skyline clear as crystal suddenly took on bright silhouettes. Waves of light slowly gave up their detail—figures (with faces?) set in droves upon droves, each lifting holy spears up into the ether. Completely silent . . . and yet roaring. How would that servant's eyes have responded? What would his chest have felt? Tears and heartbeats—that's what I imagine. I imagine him breathless and burgeoning into the boldness that only faith can give. It takes *faith* to perceive God's spoken presence, remember? What a gift of faith that moment must have been!

The story of Elisha's servant brings up an important point: we're not *always* deceived, are we? We don't always believe the great lie. The psalmist shows wondrous awareness of God's presence when he writes, "Where shall I go from your Spirit? Or where shall I flee from your presence? If I ascend to heaven, you are there! If I take the wings of the morning and dwell in the uttermost parts of the sea, even there your hand shall lead me, and your right hand shall hold me" (Ps. 139:7–9). Oh yes, the great lie doesn't have constant domain by any means. God hasn't just revealed his presence consistently throughout history; he's also helped his creatures perceive it in grace. That work of grace, warring against the great lie, has never ceased. And when grace incarnate (Jesus Christ) came to us, God gave the serpent of the great lie a deadly blow.

Still, acknowledging God's presence seems to be the exception in Scripture, not the norm. The purpose of this chapter was to offer some representative examples from the Old Testament. Many more could be offered, both there and in the New Testament, but I'll direct readers elsewhere for more discussion on that.[4]

In the chapters ahead, we'll examine different facets of our own lives and how those facets reflect our rebellion against God's presence. But before we begin exploring this, I want to remind us *why* the serpent's great lie has been so potent.

The Potency of Suggestion

Deceit's greatest asset is subtlety. I don't think Eve would have listened to the serpent if verses 1–3 weren't in the Bible. Go directly to opposition, and few will be moved. But go indirectly to it, and the whole world will follow.

---

4. I recommend the fine introduction by Lanier Burns, *The Nearness of God: His Presence with His People*, Explorations in Biblical Theology (Phillipsburg, NJ: P&R, 2009).

Lies are most believable when they come closest to the truth.

Yet, the serpent was more crafty than using indirectness. As we noted, the serpent's decision to speak as if God weren't present was a decision to work invisibly. Much of the time, we focus on the content of the serpent's speech, on what he said rather than on how he said it. That, I argue, is what makes the lie so potent, so deceptive.

My reasoning goes something like this. Lies are most believable when they come closest to the truth. The truer something appears, the more easily people will be deceived. And the serpent's speech appeared to be "mere speech." In other words, he acted *as if* language itself was neutral, a medium that is used in the same way by everyone. That's false. Nothing in creation is neutral. It's either *for* God or *against* him. God didn't finish creation and see that it was "very neutral." He saw that it was "very good." Language, as part of God's creation, was "good," not neutral. But in Genesis 3, the serpent is acting as if language can be uttered in neutrality, as if the *matter* of speech had nothing to do with *the nature* of the speaker (the father of lies). That is where the serpent's deception began. That's why the great lie is so potent.

Words and Character

Whenever we utter words, we do so in a way that reflects our nature and character. This is partly because thoughts and motives are always beneath the speech we utter. Jesus said that every person speaks "out of the abundance of the heart" (Luke 6:45). The heart and mind are reservoirs from which speech is drawn. In this sense, there's no such thing as "mere speech," as neutrality in language. C. S. Lewis was right: "*mere* is always a dangerous word."[5] A certain *mannerism* is always present in language—not just the *what* of content but the *how* of delivery, which is based on thoughts and motives of the heart. The manner of speech is monumentally important.

In light of these truths, we always speak *as if*. We always have thoughts and motives shaping our discourse. There's no such thing as "mere speech."

Now, one of the more basic thoughts or motives that shape our speech is the one we've been considering: the belief that God is present with us. This is joined to many other basic theological beliefs, beliefs in all of God's other attributes. But I focus on this one because it has epic implications for our spiritual lives. It has the potential to put us on a path of rebellion against God's presence. When the serpent spoke *as if* God were not present, Adam and Eve followed in his footsteps. And we're often doing the same. It's time to leave that path.

So far, I've discussed the great lie in terms of its origin and potency. We've seen the great lie as an assault on God's presence. We've also seen Satan assault that presence in Genesis 3, Job 1–2, and Matthew 4. In doing so, Satan introduced a path of rebellion against God's presence that Scripture illustrates in

---

5. C. S. Lewis, *The Four Loves* (New York: HarperCollins, 2017), "Introduction," Kindle.

many Old Testament figures (Cain, Jacob, Abraham, Elisha's servant, to name just a few). Eventually, we'll see the biblical solution, the better path of faithfulness, set for us by the incarnate feet of God. But before that, let's explore how the great lie has damaged many areas of our lives. Noting these areas will make it very clear what sort of solution we need, the solution Jesus Christ provides for us in the Spirit.

Reflection Questions and Prayer

1. Think of a time when you were ignorant of God's presence. What was the result of that ignorance?
2. Think of a time when you seemed aware of God's presence. What was the result of that awareness?
3. In what ways do you see people in your own life speaking *as if* God were not present?
4. What is something you or another Christian has said in which the *manner* of speech was just as important as the *matter*?
5. Choose an area of your life where you seem to act *as if* God were not present. Pray to the Spirit that he would open your eyes. Then take notes that week on how that prayer is being answered. You'll need to keep yourself rooted in God's word throughout the week.

Prayer

God, I hate the history of ignorance
That we've written under you.

We're so unaware of something so obvious.
Forgive us in Christ Jesus,
And draw us into the truth of *who* and *where* you are.
Help us to become more aware of your presence
So that we can think, speak, and act
As children before the glowing face of God.

6
THE WORLD AND GOD'S PRESENCE

In the previous chapters, we laid the theological groundwork for our discussion. We've looked at the great lie as an attack on God's presence, introduced by Satan and propagated by God's creatures. Central to all that we've discussed is the biblical truth of God's spoken presence, which is where we started.

God is present in the world through his word, which includes *creation speech* and *special speech*. The latter is the only speech that leads to salvation, and we need God's *special speech* to interpret what *creation speech* is telling us about him. Satan, however, wants none of this. He wants us to live *as if* God were not present through his authoritative word. At best, Satan wants us to think, speak, and act as if God's presence were irrelevant. It's no exaggeration to say that most people today live under the haze of the great lie.

The question we're looking at in this chapter is this: what has happened to the world as a result of the great lie? Put differently, how has the world been affected by the assumption that God isn't present, the assumption that we're on our own? We'll look at this question in the following pages. Then we'll look at how the great lie has affected our thoughts, words, and actions. And that will put us in the perfect place to receive God's great answer to the great lie.

The World's Experience?

Rocks, trees, valleys, grass, flowers, air, water—these aren't personal things, and so they can't *experience* the fall and the great lie as we can, right? Like most assumptions, that's true in one sense, false in another. The inanimate parts of the world don't have a soul; they don't need to confess Christ as Lord in order to be saved. They aren't *persons*. And yet, as elements breathed out, governed, and sustained by God's personal word, the world is far more personal than we realize. And it's certainly affected by our personal decisions.

Scripture is full of *personifications*—personal language used to describe inanimate things—when it comes to nature, the things we label as purely physical or biological. Blood "cries" (Gen. 4:10). Waters "see" and "tremble" (Ps. 77:16). Rivers "clap their hands," and hills "sing" (Ps. 98:8). The sun can be "ashamed" (Isa. 24:23). The Son of God himself says that the rocks will "cry out" if the people are silent (Luke 19:40). The Apostle Paul says that all creation is "groaning" in birth pains (Rom. 8:22). The whole world is "waiting" for the revelation of the sons of God (Rom. 8:19). What's going on here?

Some people say, "It's just personification," as if that response answered the question. It doesn't, really. Personification is a literary technique—that's true. It can be used to give a more personal feel to the thing or atmosphere being described. The question is, *why did God choose to use it?* He could have recorded everything in Scripture literally and mechanically, but he didn't. He chose to use personification. Why?

That's a deep and mysterious question that I frankly don't

have an answer to. But I can at least say this: God meant to use that language rather than literal or technical language. And the fact that he meant to do this tells me that there's something this language communicates that literal or technical language can't. What, exactly?

Here's an idea. What if this personal language is meant to help us realize our bond with the rest of creation? In the beginning, God told us to tend the garden, "to work it and keep it" (Gen. 2:15). The natural world was given as part of our divinely-bestowed purpose. God is saying, "This is why you are here. This is what you're supposed to do." Creation wasn't something to be manipulated or exploited. It was meant to be worked and *kept*. The Hebrew word used here (*shamar*), meaning to *guard* or *keep*, elsewhere in Scripture has connotations of personal protection. It's used for watchmen, gatekeepers, and even bodyguards. The range of meaning for this verb suggests we're tied to the rest of creation by God's own bidding in order to protect it, to watch over it, to keep it safe. The personifications throughout Scripture may serve to complement that watching relationship, showing how intimately we're tied to the created world. We *were* made from its base substance, after all. We came *from* it in order to look *after* it. In Herman Bavinck's words, mankind must "watch over it, safeguard it, protect it against all evil that may threaten it, must, in short, secure it against the service of corruption in which the whole of creation now groans."[1] (Given Romans 8:22, it's clear we failed at this.)

---

1. Herman Bavinck, *The Wonderful Works of God: Instruction in the Christian Religion according to the Reformed Confession*, trans. Henry Zylstra (Glenside, PA: Westminster

This is tied to God's word being his presence, since that word is what he used to create all things. Burns sets it out plainly.

> The Bible begins with God's creation of the heavens and the earth. His presence was expressed as his creative Word that ordered life on earth, "And God said . . . and there was." . . . The image of God, among other nuances, established humanity's role on the earth, personal affinity with God, and the possibility of receiving revelation and communicating in prayer. In a word, *it bonded people and the rest of creation to the relational presence of the Creator forever*, for blessing or curse.[2]

God's word, expressing his relational presence, is what binds us to the created world. We have an intimate, God-given relationship with all that God has made. We can't exist without the rest of creation. It flows into our bodies: air, water, apple skins, sugar cane. We literally take the natural world *into* ourselves. And when we die, our remains become part of the natural world again. We are *so* connected with the world God has made! We're so connected, in fact, that what happens to *us* has implications for *the world*.

The World and the Great Lie

What does all this have to do with the great lie? Look around you. What do you see as you drive, as you walk, as the weather

---

Seminary Press, 2019), 169.

2. Lanier Burns, *The Nearness of God: His Presence with His People*, Explorations in Biblical Theology (Phillipsburg, NJ: P&R, 2009), 41; emphasis added.

shifts and the seasons drift into each other?

I'm a runner—not the marathon type, though. I run a few miles, multiple times a week, when I'm disciplined. As my feet pad along the edge of the roads winding like ribbons through the Pennsylvania countryside, I look at the fields. I see the fallow rows of old corn, the white-gold spines singing of summer past. I see the golden rod and milkweed content to swish as unnoticing cars graze them with carried wind. I see the front lawns, each curated with a thousand little intentions from God's image bearers—some with beards and little potbellies; some with wise, gray hair catching the sun; some with full resolve to keep the grass trim and clean. These are people working and keeping their little garden plots on God's broad-faced country.

I see the big, black bodies of turkey vultures, casting their menacing shadows from lordly heights down on the mice and voles in the fields. If I'm lucky, I'll see my favorite creature swirling in loops on a thermal: the red-tailed hawk. I always stop to stare at them. They seem . . . noble in some ancient sense, keeping the blue jays and robins and chickadees beneath them.

I smell the must of overturned earth. It calls to me quietly, just wanting recognition that *I* came from *it*. I was gathered from sediment and soil. It was the breath of God that made dust dream and dance and drink. God, I think, is in the grand practice of making something from nothing (Rom. 4:17), even though we think nothing of his somethings.

And then I see . . . a Budweiser can bent in half. Then a shining, blue chip bag padded into the dirt and grit. Then a plastic bottle of cheap whiskey. Then the brown bottom of a beer bottle crushed into the gravel, shaped like a waxing gibbous moon.

When a truck passes me, I hold my breath for three seconds so I don't take the gray-black exhaust into my lungs. It doesn't work all that well. I still taste sulfur and burnt oil.

Why is there this dissonance—between birds and bottles, milkweed and motor oil, shards of rubber and sheaves of corn? Because of the great lie.

In God's worded world, his spoken presence is always before us. But the great lie encourages those who were meant to *keep* and *protect* God's world to live *as if* he weren't present, that no authoritative judgment would follow the ravaging of God's garden. Can you see where I'm going?

The great lie has made many people treat the world as if God weren't present, as if lives are free to litter, and that matters.

It's always better when we're candid with each other, so let me start there. I'm not an environmentalist or a roof-top shouting climate change advocate. I have my own beliefs about those issues, but that's not what I'm focusing on in this chapter. This isn't a political appeal. It's a report of heart-sadness.

My heart is saddened when I see the garbage on the roadside. It's a bit like seeing soda spilled on a Thomas Cole painting. Things created, sustained, and governed by the speech of God are being spit on; they're corroding under our neglect. The great lie has made many people treat the world as if God weren't present, as if lives are free to litter, and that matters.

Given the tie we have with creation, what happens to *us* has an effect on *the world*. When we believe in the great lie, when we act *as if* God weren't present in the fields and skies, behind every sheaf of corn and beneath every red-tailed wing, creation suffers. In fact, it *groans*.

The Groaning of the World

Look at Paul's language in Romans 8:18–25.

> [18] For I consider that the sufferings of this present time are not worth comparing with the glory that is to be revealed to us. [19] For the creation waits with eager longing for the revealing of the sons of God. [20] For the creation was subjected to futility, not willingly, but because of him who subjected it, in hope [21] that the creation itself will be set free from its bondage to corruption and obtain the freedom of the glory of the children of God. [22] For we know that the whole creation has been groaning together in the pains of childbirth until now. [23] And not only the creation, but we ourselves, who have the firstfruits of the Spirit, groan inwardly as we wait eagerly for adoption as sons, the redemption of our bodies. [24] For in this hope we were saved. Now hope that is seen is not hope. For who hopes for what he sees? [25] But if we hope for what we do not see, we wait for it with patience.

What's the current state of creation? Here it is in bullet points.

- Eager longing
- Futility
- Enslavement to corruption
- Groaning

Not a great depiction of the created world, is it? But did you notice the link between the state of creation and the state of humanity?

What's creation longing for? "The revealing of *the sons of God*." What sort of freedom does creation strive after? "The freedom of the glory of *the children of God*." Who is groaning? *Both* creation *and* humanity. Paul uses the same verb in verses 22 and 23. Right now, we're *hoping* and *waiting*. But that hope and wait is tied to creation. Remember: what happens to *us* has implications for *the world*.

When *we* are deceived by the great lie and act as if God weren't present, casting aside the call of Genesis 2:15, creation suffers. It's suffering right now. Those plastic bottles and chip bags on the roadside are evidence of neglect. But it's not just neglect of nature, of the created world. Read these words slowly, since we overlook this truth so habitually: *It's a deeper neglect of God's presence*. It's even a subtle attack on God's presence. To treat the world as a garbage can is to treat it in opposition to how God's word says we should treat it: to guard and protect it. God's presence demands our relational faithfulness, and part of that faithfulness is how we treat the world around us.

The world is *groaning*. It's groaning in a way that somehow mirrors how *we* are groaning for the redemption of our decaying bodies. *We* want to be made new. *Creation* wants to be made new. Creatures and God's creation are both groaning. And the great lie is partially to blame.

Love the Presence of God in the World

This brings out a biblical call for all Christians, no matter where they stand on environmentalism and climate change: we need to learn how to love God's presence in the world. It's not a matter of caring for stuff, for things, or even for "nature." It's a matter of acknowledging and respecting the presence of God, the one who lovingly and graciously spoke all things into being.

Without love for God's presence, we'll never change how we interact with the world.

Andrew Klavan wrote, "Love is the key to knowing the creation truly because creation is the act of love by a Trinity that is an eternal act of love."[3] *Love* is the key. But notice, it's not merely a love for creation. Plenty of Christians wax

3. Andrew Klavan, *Truth and Beauty: How the Lives and Works of England's Greatest Poets Point the Way to a Deeper Understanding of the Words of Jesus* (Grand Rapids, MI: Zondervan, 2022), 216.

on about how much they love "nature." I don't know half as many who specifically say they love *the presence of God* in nature. There's a big difference. Nature is not just stuff, things made for us to gaze at, engage with, and (sadly) manipulate or exploit. Nature is a living, breathing manifestation of God's presence, his *spoken presence*. And without love for God's presence, we'll never change how we interact with the world.

You see, it's not just "sin" that's responsible for the brokenness and abuse of the natural world. While that's true broadly, it doesn't move us much, does it? Carl Trueman once told us in a church history class, "General answers tell us almost nothing specifically. If someone asks, 'Why did the two towers collapse on 9/11?' And you answered, 'Gravity,' that would be correct. But it wouldn't tell us much." The point is that we need specific answers to help us target a problem and response. I'm arguing that the great lie—that God is not present with us, or that his presence is irrelevant—is responsible for the groaning of creation. It's a disdain and neglect of God's presence that's the problem, and a love for God's presence is the solution.

Our complicity in the great lie, as a tacit attack on God's presence in his spoken world, is responsible for the damages we see around us. And this is the case because what happens to *us* has an effect on *the world*. Regardless of what you think politically, that's a biblical truth the Apostle Paul won't let us escape. It's a love for God's presence that stands behind our guarding and keeping of God's grand garden. It's an attack on God's presence that stands behind the groanings of that garden. We are linked to creation. What happens to us affects what happens to the world.

In the chapters ahead, we'll look at how the great lie has damaged more than the world: it's damaged our thoughts, words, and actions.

Reflection Questions and Prayer

1. Is the idea that we are tied to creation, that what happens to us has implications for it, new to you? How does it help you notice how the world might be groaning around you?

2. What are the benefits and dangers of believing in environmentalism *without* having a biblical basis for it, such as the one Paul provides in Romans?

3. In what ways do you see creation groaning around you? How is the great lie related to these ways?

4. What are some ways in which we can show a love for God's presence concretely in the world around us?

Prayer

God, you spoke the world.
When you put us in the garden,
You tied us to creation.
You called us to watch over and keep it.
We have failed.
What's happened in our hearts,
Our rebellion against your presence,
Has affected creation.

Give us a love for your presence,
A constant awareness of it,
So that we can care for the world
In which you are always present.
Help each of us to stand on love for you
As we seek to watch over and guard the world again.
Spirit, show us how to bring the redemption of Christ
To a world that is groaning for us.

Reader Resource: Learning More about the World

There are many resources out there that can help you learn more about the world and its brokenness. Here are just some of the ones I've consulted and found helpful.

- Herman Bavinck, *The Wonderful Works of God: Instruction in the Christian Religion according to the Reformed Confession*, trans. Henry Zylstra (Glenside, PA: Westminster Seminary Press, 2019), 111–125.
- William Boekestein, "Why Should I Care about Animals?" The Gospel Coalition, March 9, 2022, https://www.thegospelcoalition.org/article/care-animals-jonah/.
- John Frame, *Nature's Case for God: A Brief Biblical Argument* (Bellingham, WA: Lexham, 2018), chap. 5, "The Presence."
- John Frame, *Systematic Theology: An Introduction to Christian Belief* (Phillipsburg, NJ: P&R, 2013), 383–389.

- Jonathan Merritt, R. Albert Mohler Jr., and Cal Beisner, "Green Plus Christian Isn't New Math," *Christianity Today*, June 30, 2010, https://www.christianitytoday.com/ct/2010/june/26.46.html.
- "The Joyful Environmentalists: Eugene Peterson and Peter Harris," *Christianity Today*, June 17, 2011, https://www.christianitytoday.com/ct/2011/june/joyfulenvironment.html.
- John Piper, "The Pleasure of God in His Creation," Desiring God, February 8, 1987, https://www.desiringgod.org/messages/the-pleasure-of-god-in-his-creation.
- Vern S. Poythress, "He Makes the Wind Blow," *World Magazine*, May 31, 2008, https://wng.org/articles/he-makes-the-wind-blow-1617335765.
- Vern S. Poythress, "Visible Things: Their Origin, Nature, and Purpose," The Works of John Frame & Vern Poythress, September 26, 2020, https://frame-poythress.org/visible-things-their-origin-nature-and-purpose/.
- Vern S. Poythress, *The Mystery of the Trinity: A Trinitarian Approach to the Attributes of God* (Phillipsburg, NJ: P&R 2020), 43–48.

7
OUR THOUGHTS AND GOD'S PRESENCE

W e now move from the outside (the damaged world) to the inside (our damaged thoughts). It's easy for us to assume that thoughts are "mere thoughts." But remember what C.S. Lewis said: *mere* is a dangerous word. What if thoughts aren't just free-floating mind clouds, uncontrollable elements of the soul's weather? What if they're more like crystals? What if they can be fractured, broken, and clouded with impurities? And what if we're called to inspect them? More importantly, what if we're meant to have God's truth *redeem* them?

Our Thought and God's Presence

Let's start by applying the truth we've been discussing throughout the book: God is always and everywhere present. That means he's present in our minds. As the psalmist writes,

> You know when I sit down and when I rise up;
>   you discern my thoughts from afar.
> You search out my path and my lying down
>   and are acquainted with all my ways.
> Even before a word is on my tongue,
>   behold, O Lord, you know it altogether. (Ps. 139:2–4)

God discerns your thoughts—even before they enter your mind. He sees them as distant comets careening towards your consciousness. He knows what you think before you think it, since he's present in every space, both outside you and within you. Just as God is always in the room, he's always in your head.

We hold the delusion that our mind is a fortress that keeps everyone out but us. But that's just an offshoot of the great lie. If all of creation reveals God's spoken presence, and we're a part of creation, then every part of us reveals the presence of God, the one who upholds our brainwaves by the word of his power (Heb. 1:3). God sees everything in your head. You think before a divine audience. And God reveals himself in even the darkest and smallest cloisters of your thought.

Our Thought and God's Word

God's presence in our minds runs counter to the great lie. Remember, if God won't be true to his own word, if God won't be present to judge, then the world is an abandoned playground. We're all running around without supervision and without direction. In that scenario, thoughts can't even be good or bad; they just happen. They're just brain waves, since there's no objective means to weigh them.

But, thank God, the world is *not* an abandoned playground. It's a divine estate. We're living and moving and breathing on someone else's property. And just as what happens *to* us has implications for the world—the divine estate—what happens *inside* us has implications for our souls.

The mind is a potent weapon in the war between God and

Satan. That's one of the reasons why we're called to take every *thought* captive to Christ (2 Cor. 10:5). It's a war that's already been won in Christ, but the devil won't give up on his daily skirmishes. And he knows that if he can get inside our heads, he can wreak havoc. As Jennie Allen wrote, "If our thought lives are the deepest, darkest places of stronghold within us, all hell will try to stop us from being free."[1] Conversely, if Christ, the truth, is in our head, we'll know the peace and presence of God. We'll know that God is with us *always* (Matt. 28:20).

We'll get to Christ in a few chapters. For now, let's look at how the great lie assaults our minds.

The underlying assault is tied directly to the great lie. If the great lie is that God isn't present with us, then that would mean we're on our own. We're independent. Theologians call this *autonomy*. In the Greek, the word breaks down to *self law*. You can see how problematic this is for creatures made to be dependent on the God who gives. John Frame put it this way:

> Sinners at heart do not want to live in God's world, though they have no choice about it. They recognize the truth to some extent, because they need to get along and to make a living. But they would very much like the world to be different, and often they either try to make it different or pretend that it is. In the unbelieving fantasy world, the Lord of the Bible does not exist, and man is free to live by his own standards of truth and right. In a word, the unbeliever lives as if he

---

1. Jennie Allen, *Get Out of Your Head: Stopping the Spiral of Toxic Thoughts* (Colorado Springs, CO: WaterBrook, 2020), 35. Kindle edition.

were *autonomous*, subject only to his own law. Nobody can be really autonomous, because we are all subject to God's control, authority, and presence. But we pretend that we are autonomous; we act as though we were autonomous, in the unbelieving fantasy world.[2]

An unbelieving fantasy world—that's the world people try to live in when they believe the great lie. It's a false world.

The Dutch Reformed theologian Cornelius Van Til (1895–1987) spent much of his time attacking this lie of human autonomy, especially as it relates to our thought. The assumption in the broader philosophical world is that thought has nothing to do with God or good or evil. The reasoning we use on a daily basis is just a tool, like a butter knife or a screwdriver.

Van Til would have none of that. He knew we live in the presence of God, both outside us and inside us. And what he said about our thought is striking. He talked about sinful man as "the natural man" or the "non-regenerate man" in the following quote. Non-regenerate just means "not reborn in the Spirit" (John 3). The quote may seem intimidating, but we'll unpack what we need from it.

The natural man wants to be something that he cannot be. He wants to be "as God," himself the judge of good and evil, himself the standard of truth. He sets himself as the ideal

---

2. John M. Frame, *A History of Western Philosophy and Theology* (Phillipsburg, NJ: P&R, 2015), 22.

of *comprehensive* knowledge. When he sees that he will never reach this ideal, he concludes that all reality is surrounded by darkness. As a child would say, "If I cannot do this, no one else can," so the "natural man" today says in effect that, since he cannot grasp knowledge comprehensively, God cannot either. The non-regenerate man takes for granted that the meaning of the space-time world is immanent in itself, and that man is the ultimate interpreter of this world, instead of its humble interpreter. The natural man wants to be creatively constructive instead of receptively reconstructive.[3]

That last line is critical even if it sounds cryptic. "Creatively constructive" means, "I decide what's true or false, real or unreal. I build my own world." The biblical opposite is to be "receptively reconstructive." That means we come to know what's true by *receiving* and *submitting* to God's revelation, his *special speech*.

So, what happens when we *don't* receive or submit to that revelation? Non-Christians would say, "Nothing." Faithful Christians must say, "Everything." If we don't look to God's word in order to understand who God is, who we are, and what the world is like, then we'll see everything askew, like looking through a frost-covered window in winter. We see colors and shapes, shades of light and darkness, but we can't truly see what's there with any certainty or definition.

---

3. Cornelius Van Til, *An Introduction to Systematic Theology: Prolegomena and the Doctrines of Revelation, Scripture*, and God, 2nd ed., ed. William Edgar (Phillipsburg, NJ: P&R, 2007), 63.

Now, why all this focus on autonomy, knowledge, and revelation? Because the great lie is at the center of it. Remember that the serpent's lie in the garden was meant to get Adam and Eve to act *as if* they were independent, as if God weren't really present to judge with authority. That lie has bled into the soil of our thought. We begin *assuming* that God isn't present, often because we can't *feel* him, and we'd prefer feelings to thoughts, since feelings are so much easier to respond to. Jared Wilson wrote, "The devil wants us only feeling our feelings, not thinking about them. His playground is the visible world of experience and reaction. If you start thinking beyond what you see and feel, you might somehow stumble into faith, and he certainly can't have that."[4]

God's word always confronts and corrects our thought.

Because God is an invisible Spirit, we don't experience him in the same way we experience the world. But God has revealed himself to us, he's given us the truth and authority of his word, so that we can walk the straight and narrow path. Walking on that path will mean we often combat or reinterpret our feelings in light of what God says. We may *feel* autonomous, but we're completely dependent on God. "I am the vine; you are the branches. Whoever abides in me and I in him, he it is

---

4. Jared C. Wilson, *The Gospel according to Satan: Eight Lies about God That Sound Like the Truth* (Nashville, TN: Nelson, 2020), 73–74.

that bears much fruit, for apart from me you can do nothing" (John 15:5). We may *feel* alone, but we're surrounded by God. "Where shall I go from your Spirit? Or where shall I flee from your presence?" (Ps. 139:7) We may *feel* as if God isn't with us, but we live, breathe, and move *in* him (Acts 17:28). God's word always confronts and corrects our thought. It also demands that our feelings submit to him, like wild dogs coming to heel.

Thoughts Can Be Evil

I mentioned that Cornelius Van Til fought vehemently against the notion that our thoughts are neutral. God's *world* isn't neutral. God's world is a divine estate, permeated by his presence, and we're responsible for whatever we do on it. That includes our thoughts, which are drawn from experience within this world. When a thought we have clashes with the truth of God's revealed word, a battle ensues—even if it lasts half a second. And it's actually a battle between good and evil, God and Satan, the great truth that God is present with us and the great lie that he's absent. Thoughts, in other words, can be evil.

One of the many telling lines in C. S. Lewis's *The Screwtape Letters* is this one, from one devil to another, "It is funny how mortals always picture us as putting things into their minds: in reality our best work is done by keeping them out" (Letter 4). Keeping what out of our minds, exactly? Here's one example: the idea that thoughts can be evil or demonic, that they can wage war against the authoritative presence of God.

I realize in our contemporary secularized culture, where everything has been de-supernaturalized, that's a lot to take in.

"Aren't thoughts just . . . *thoughts*? Synapses firing in the brain? You don't have to go all medieval on something that has a perfectly grounded medical and scientific explanation." I hear you. Really, I do.

But what if that is *exactly* what demons want? Screwtape told his nephew that they do their "best work" by keeping things *out* of our heads, not putting things into them. What if they've been celebrating since the Enlightenment (and well before that) because of a truth they've kept *out* of our heads, convincing people of God's absence in our thought life, chanting the refrain that thought is just a neutral, physiological phenomenon? What if Satan celebrates the fact that many Christians view their thought lives as neutral?

I'm reminded of a similar *what if* that John Mark Comer draws out, as he builds on the work of Evagrius (a monk of the early church) in *Live No Lies*.

> For Evagrius, *logosmoi,* or our thought patterns, are the primary vehicle of demonic attack upon our souls. That might sound far-fetched to our skeptical Western ears, but think about it: Have you ever had a thought (or feeling or desire) that seemed to have a will to it? An agenda that was hard to resist? And not thinking it felt like fighting gravity? It seemed to have a weight or power over you that was beyond your ability to resist?
>
> Could it be that the thoughts that assault your mind's peace aren't *just* thoughts? Could it be that a dark, animating energy is behind them? A spiritual force?

Could it be that this is about more than mental hygiene or positive thinking; it's about resistance?[5]

"A dark, animating energy". . . What if thoughts *aren't* just synapses firing within the soft walls of our brain tissue? What if a thought could be *weaponized*—for good or evil? Would that change the way we walk through life each day?

I think it would. And doesn't this make a bit more sense out of Paul's call to spiritual warfare in Ephesians 6:12? We're fighting against things that sound pretty abstract to 21st century Western ears: cosmic powers and spiritual forces of evil. And that's not just a fraction of the enemy; that's *the* enemy. Our war isn't against "flesh and blood"; it's against *this*.

"Hold up," says the well-rounded Christian skeptic (is that an oxymoron?). "How can you possibly link *thoughts* with these things?" Well, think about what our spiritual enemies *do*. Then think about what a thought can do. Satan and his servants want to do essentially three things. Notice how each of these things is related to a war against the presence of God.

Satan and his minions want to take us . . .

1. *Further from God.* We only move in two different directions: either towards God (towards his personal/spiritual presence) or towards Satan. That's it. There's no neutral zone. Moving in God's direction means moving deeper into a personal relationship with him so that we start

---

5. John Mark Comer, *Live No Lies: Recognize and Resist the Three Enemies That Sabotage Your Peace* (Colordo Springs, CO: WaterBrook, 2021), 86.

to resemble our creative, loving, generous, patient, self-giving Lord. Moving in Satan's direction means becoming a black hole for all goodness. We become destructive, malevolent, hoarding, quick-tempered, self-seeking centers of chaos.

2. *Deeper into doubt.* If Satan can get you to doubt God and his promises, to doubt God's authoritative *presence* in your thoughts, then he's already won the hardest part of the battle. Genesis 3 is a case in point. Doubting God's presence was something that happened *inside* people, and this led immediately to breaking God's law, which led to death and a kingdom of curses.

3. *Lower into self-absorption.* The devil's aim is to bend our backs so much that we stare at ourselves for eternity. In that sense, it's not so much that Satan wants to convince us that God isn't *present*; it's that he wants us to think that God's presence is irrelevant. He wants each one of us to be as self-absorbed as possible, the practical center of our fantasy universe, a universe in which God's presence makes no difference to us.

Now, if a *thought* does one of these things—if it takes us further from God, deeper into doubt, or lower in self-absorption—wouldn't you feel comfortable classifying it as a weapon of the enemy, an agent of evil? And if a thought does the opposite of one of these, wouldn't it be an agent of God, giving power to his presence?

"But how do you know the difference between an evil

thought and a sinful thought or a plain old synapse firing?" That's an important question. There are plenty of passages in the Old and New Testaments to help us identify evil as such. One of the most helpful to me recently has been Romans 14:23. "Whatever does not proceed from faith is sin." A lustful thought, for instance, even for your spouse, does not proceed from faith. So, you can identify that thought as sin. But what about identifying it as *evil*?

Though it's not a fail-proof method, in addition to paying attention to the criteria above, we would do well to note the *persistence* of the thought. Does the thought keep coming back, over and over again? Does it seem to bind you with invisible chains, drawing you away constantly from God, pushing you to doubt, encouraging self-focus? Chances are, that's evil.

Consider the man Jesus encountered in the country of the Gerasenes in Mark 5 (also in Matt. 8 and Luke 8). This was a man bound *persistently* by evil, so much so that no one could even cross his path. He spent his days bursting through chains, crying out to the landscape, and cutting himself with stones. He was a man of curses, chaos, and blood. Surely, this was drawing him always further from God, deeper into doubt and despair, and lower into self-absorption. And this became not just a frequent occurrence, but his *life*. It consumed him.

And look at what it says after Jesus cast out the demons from him and sent them into a herd of pigs. He was sitting with Jesus (closer to God), clothed (trusting in God's provision), and "in his *right mind*," able to recognize and acknowledge others (5:15). If he was in his "right mind" after Jesus healed him, then he was in his "wrong mind" before that. His thought life was evil. But Jesus made it right. Jesus made it good.

So, can a thought be evil? It sure can be. That's a truth Screwtape and his progeny would rather keep out of your head. And maybe the great lie is the most evil thought in human history. When we encounter it, we need to combat it with the truth of God's presence.

Combating Evil Thoughts

How do we combat evil thoughts, including the great lie? We kill them. Sorry if that sounds too violent, but it's the only way. We kill evil thoughts with powerful truth. More specifically, we rehearse hand-selected Scripture whenever the evil thought approaches. The word of God isn't just a conceptual comfort; it's a cutting blade. It cuts through evil. When we're struggling to fight a particular thought, we need to confront that thought with the power of the truth. If thoughts can be evil, then they can also be wise and righteous; they can be Christ-exalting. They can honor the presence of God and *change* us accordingly.

Let's look at a few variations of the great lie and how we might combat them. This will put us in a good place to discuss how the great lie has affected our words, which emerge from our thoughts. For each of the lies below, we'll look at what's beneath it and how the truth of God's word responds to it by affirming his presence.[6]

God isn't really here. The key word here is "really." What do we

_____

6. This is the approach Comer sets out in *Live No Lies.*

mean by it? We might mean we can't perceive God's presence. We might mean that God doesn't see what's happening to us or what we're doing. We might mean that there aren't any consequences for the words and actions surrounding us. In all cases, "really" suggests there's a certain way in which we want to perceive God's presence—perhaps some physical means (sight, sense, spiritual fervor or conviction). When we don't perceive God in the way we want, we're prone to believe the lie. And that starts to affect our words and actions. Remember Eve. After the serpent twisted God's words, Eve responded with an exaggeration. "Neither shall you touch it" (Gen. 3:3). God never said anything about "touching." Eve's thoughts were moving in the wrong direction, towards Satan. This is reflected in her words (the subject of the next chapter). When we're tempted, as Adam and Eve were, to think that God isn't really here, that he's not revealing himself in the way we'd like him to, we're called to focus our attention on the way in which he is really here, for instance, through his *spoken presence*. If God has told us that he's revealed himself in all the things that he's made, then we can look around us and see God's presence mediated through creation. Everything we see has something to say about God (creation speech). And when we struggle to perceive God's presence that way, we always have God's verbal address to us in Scripture. Scripture isn't just God's word; it's God's word *to us*, to his people, to his church. When we want to hear God's voice, we can open his word to hear it. We can listen with our eyes. When we read passages such as Ps. 9:9–10; Ps. 97:5; Ps. 139:7–12; Matt. 28:20; Eph. 2:18 and many others, we can *know* that God is present. Our minds can grasp what our feelings cannot. God is really here. He's speaking to you. He's never stopped, in fact. God's revelation in nature and in Scripture is a ceaseless song. It's always playing; we just aren't good at listening. God's word reminds us to listen. And the Spirit will work to help us hear.

God's presence isn't authoritative for you. Most people would never be this brazen, but we might *act* as if this lie were true. This form of the great lie has a clear tie to Genesis 3, since it was the authority of God that Satan directly challenged. We can fall into believing the same lie. The lie says, in essence, "Okay, well God might be present, but he's not authoritative. He's not going to *judge* me for stealing a pack of gum from the drugstore register." God's authoritative presence is linked to his word, which is covenantal. That word makes promises—to curse or to bless, to judge or uphold. Just like Adam and Eve, we're often tempted to believe this lie because judgment doesn't come on our timeline. We think that if judgment isn't immediate, then it's not there.

When I was a kid, I stole a baseball from the local convenience store. It was before the time of security tags and alarms at exit doors. I walked out the exit with that ball safely in my sweatshirt pocket. Nothing happened. I got away with it. Well . . . until my dad found out what I did. Then came the remorse, and the trip back to the store, where I handed the baseball back and apologized for what I did. The lady at the customer service desk seemed surprised that we were taking this whole thing so seriously. But my dad was a man of

God. He knew I'd done evil, and he wasn't going to let it slide. God was present authoritatively in this scenario, even though I didn't perceive it. He was present in my conscience, in my warring guilt and greed, in my watchful father. Just because God's authority isn't immediately apparent doesn't mean God isn't there. *He's always there.* And his righteousness has saturated our conscience. We can't escape the longing for it or the regret when we fall short. Nor should we miss the joy when we see that Christ *is* our righteousness (1 Cor. 1:30). God is always authoritatively present and beautifully encouraging in Christ Jesus, whose Spirit burns in us.

God's presence isn't a safety net; it's a pair of glasses.

God is irrelevant. This might be one of the most destructive lies of our time. To say that God is irrelevant isn't only saying, "He doesn't matter." It's also saying, "His presence is pointless." People have the hardest time not simply deciding to believe in God but, after they've decided to believe, to see how that belief makes any difference in their lives. God can be little more than a pleasant *idea* to people, a safety net to land on when trauma pushes them over the edge. But if that's all God's presence means to people, their faith will shrivel up and blow away in the wind. Like an autumn leaf that was brilliant red for a season, their hope will brown and ossify, ending up on the sidewalk of life, a testament to what beauty *used* to be.

But God's presence isn't a safety net; it's a pair of glasses.

We see the world differently when we believe that God is present. A stop sign may appear to be nothing more than a piece of metal covered in reflective paint. But if God is present and communes with us, it can be much more. I'll never forget how I tried to push back my tears as a teenager, right after we learned my father would die of cancer in a matter of weeks. I kept trying to reassure my mom and offer some consolation. I kept my foot to the pedal in the hospital parking lot, as if the movement would help me get past the biting grief. And then I looked up: A stop sign in the middle of the parking lot was a call from the Spirit. "Just stop. Stop. It's okay to stay here. It's okay to fall apart." And I broke down and wept at that stop sign. God is never irrelevant. He takes the seemingly menial and gives it meaning. In fact, he gives *everything* meaning.[7] And what could irrelevance be except an absence of meaning? The meaning of every single dust particle and water molecule in our cosmos is bound to its purpose—the purpose of glorifying the God who speaks life and love into what he's made, and who does so because he's ever-present with us. No part of the cosmos can be meaningless if it's all created, governed, and sustained by God.

For years since this stop sign incident, I've kept the Gospel of John close, especially John 14:1–3. "Let not your hearts be

---

7. "What is true with respect to the existence of the whole space-time world is equally true with respect to the meaning of it. As the absolute and independent existence of God determines the derivative existence of the universe, so the absolute meaning that God has for himself implies that the meaning of every fact in the universe must be related to God." Van Til, *An Introduction to Systematic Theology*, 58.

troubled. Believe in God; believe also in me. In my Father's house are many rooms. If it were not so, would I have told you that I go to prepare a place for you? And if I go and prepare a place for you, I will come again and will take you to myself, that where I am you may be also." My father is just in his room now, wonderfully aware of God's presence. That truth assaults the lie that God isn't really here, with me, or with my father. It also assaults the lie that his life didn't have meaning, now that he's gone. In fact, it presses further to show that even hospital stop signs have meaning in God's plan for each of us. God is always relevant to the details in our lives.

Thoughts into Words

The great lie has bled into our thoughts for centuries upon centuries. It set us on a path of rebellion against God's word, against his spoken presence. And that's brought untold grief to countless people.

> *God's always with me—through a spoken presence that calls out for my response in prayer and worship.*

The rebellion continues today in every unchecked assumption of God's absence. Think about it for yourself. I've started the habit of waking each morning with a simple sentence on my lips: *God is here.* He's in every room—the bedroom where I sleep, the bathroom where I wash, the kitchen where I cook and eat, the sun room where I play *Pretty Pretty Princess* with my daughters. He's always with me—through a spoken presence that calls out for my response in prayer and worship. I don't see him. I don't often feel him. But I trust his speech. I take him at his word. I let his truth assault the great lie again and again and again. I do my best to take every thought captive to Christ. I make a lot of mistakes each day, but trying is the mark we aim for, not perfection. As we try faithfully, the Spirit will mature us in the faith, until our faith becomes sight.

Thoughts are deeply connected to words. So, in the next chapter, we'll look at how the great lie influences our speech.

Reflection Questions and Prayer

1. What damaging thoughts are most common for you? How does the great lie seem related to them?
2. How do your damaging thoughts affect your spiritual life?
3. What's an example of an evil thought you've had within the last week? How did you respond to it? What truth of Scripture speaks against it?
4. How often do you think of God's presence with you? Commit to saying "God is here" every time you enter a room. What difference does it make?

Prayer

God of thought and wonder,
You are truth and life and light.

Your presence surrounds me,

Though I can't see you.

You are always in the room.

Help me to sense the lies that the devil speaks,

Especially the lie of your absence.

Draw me into your fellowship

So that I trust more deeply in your speech,

Which governs and sustains all things.

May your personal presence become my greatest longing.

8
OUR WORDS AND GOD'S PRESENCE

The great lie can alter our thoughts at any point. In the previous chapter, we looked at how we respond to that great lie with the truth of Scripture, the truth of God's presence. Just as the great lie has encouraged us to assume that God is absent in our thought life, it also encourages us to speak as if he's absent. What does this look like, and how does it affect us?

A Paradise Perspective on Speech

I have this thing I do. I'm not sure where it came from, but it happens multiple times a week. Whenever I've just finished saying something to my wife or one of my kids, I imagine myself looking at that moment from galaxies away, through fields of stardust and across oceans of black, in a high and golden tower on the outskirts of paradise. In this realm, from this vantage point, everything is tempered by love, patience, and self-giving. I see myself in the orb of God's salvation, wholly safe and satisfied in God's eternal presence. I look at my earthly life from this place. And most of the time, I'm embarrassed. I mean, my heavenly self is embarrassed of my present self. Why?

I speak more harshly and have far less patience and love in my words when I'm focused on the immediate. If all I see is what's right in front of me, the smallest hills feel like mountains.

Ripples feel like rapids. A knee-scrape feels like a knife gouge. Everything is out of proportion with the glorious, blinding brilliance of my eternal salvation.

Apologies come quickly after this perspective shift. The initial embarrassment leads to repentance. And when the apology comes, it comes from that heavenly place, from my paradise perspective.

This is hard for me because I'm not naturally gifted with temperance and patience. And in these tense or troubling moments, it's not just that I forget my eternal salvation in Christ. It's that I act *as if* God weren't present with me, governing and shepherding my life with his Spirit. That, of course, is the great lie.

I can identify the great lie when I contrast my earthly life with my heavenly destiny. And this has everything to do with my appreciation of God's presence. As Jonny Gibson wrote recently in a reflection on Psalm 84, "Heaven is a praiseworthy place, but only because it is inhabited by a praiseworthy person— God. That's why this psalmist finds God's dwelling place so lovable, because the Lord of hosts, the living God, lives there. Heaven is only heaven because of who's there."[1] My paradise perspective is permeated by God's presence and my trust in the sovereign work God has woven through every detail of my life. Utterly convinced that God is ever with me and inside me, my heavenly self can put everything else in perspective, including my earthly shortcomings.

---

1. Jonathan Gibson, "Longing for Heaven, Longing for God," The Orthodox Presbyterian Church, https://opc.org/nh.html?article_id=969.

My short fuse, frustration, and sharp words on earth reveal a lack of trust in God's presence, a lack of trust in his shepherding control. If I truly trusted God's presence with me in every room, I would speak very differently. I would speak in a way that testifies to his goodness, his patience, his loving kindness. What exactly would that sort of speech look like?

Grace-Giving Words and God's Presence

Scripture is filled with insight on how we should use words. One of the most helpful to me has been Paul's instruction to the Ephesians: "Let no corrupting talk come out of your mouths, but only such as is good for building up, as fits the occasion, that it may give grace to those who hear" (Eph. 4:29). There are three qualities here, each related to our embrace of God's presence.

Good for building up. Don't take this as a call to dish out compliments. It's more than this. Why do we build others up? It's not just because "it's a nice thing to do." We build others up because we want them to know their value, their worth. We want them to see themselves anew, in the aura of God's creative and life-giving kindness. But creatures of God would have no worth apart from God's presence. We image *him*. *Our* worth is established by *his* worth. Our presence is valued because of his presence. Building others up is thus an effort in honoring God's presence through the personality of one of his creatures. We build others up not just to draw attention to their presence but to draw attention to God's presence. This may seem strange to people in our time but that's because they've functionally isolated people from their Maker. In the language of the previous chapter, they've acted as if people were *autonomous*. But that's a fantasy world. People are who they are only because God is who he is. When we build others up with our words, we affirm *both* their true, God-granted presence in this world in addition to the presence of the one who made them and continues to shepherd them by his Spirit.

As fits the occasion. This one is tough to interpret since it seems more general. What does it mean for our words to be "fitting"? Again, push past the initial assumption that this just means something generic like "appropriate." Synonyms only go so far in helping us understand meaning. If we want to use the word "appropriate" here, we'd have to say "appropriate for what?" There can't really be any such thing as "simply appropriate," as if we lived in a neutral world where everyone had the same "objective" assumptions about everything. We have to ask, "appropriate according to *what* or to *whom*?" According to the presence and purposes of God! There's too much here to get into in terms of how we might apply that to particular situations. What would you have said to me at my father's funeral? What would you have said to me on my wedding day? What would you have said to me when our firstborn came into the world? Each occasion presents us with many choices that might fall within the broad umbrella of "appropriate according to God's presence." But at the very least, we'd have to say something central about who God is. Given passages such as 1 John 4:8 and John 3:16, we could say "appropriate according to God's grace and love." What's fitting to say in any occasion has to be evocative of God's grace and love. If you passed through the funeral line after my father died, there are many things you could've say that would've fit the occasion in this sense. But "You'll get over it eventually" isn't one of them. Those words belittle the value of human life, and thus belittle the value of God's presence, who shaped and shepherded that life. But any of the following expressions would fit.

- I'm so thankful for the way your father loved the Lord.
- I'm so sorry for your loss.
- Your father was a wonderful man and gave you such a great path to follow.
- We are praying for God's comfort and peace to embrace you.
- Your father has left the shire, but you'll see him again. [A line that I didn't like at the time but have grown to love as the years pass and my appreciation for Tolkien has blossomed.]

Words that fit the occasion are those that testify to the grace and love of God, who died for those that waged war against him (Rom. 5:8). That means speaking kind words not just to friends and acquaintances but to those who deserve the opposite. In God's great grace, he saw it somehow "fitting" to speak his saving and self-sacrificing word to *us*. That should make you marvel. And it should influence your speech.

That it may give grace. This is my favorite part of the verse. Look at this divine reasoning with me. Who gives grace? God.

But what is Paul saying our words can do? Give grace. We partake in *God's* work of giving grace, through the words we utter. Isn't that amazing? The poet Malcolm Guite once wrote,

> In music, in the whole creation story,
> In his own image, his imagination,
> The Triune Poet makes us for his glory,
> And makes us each the other's inspiration.[2]

God made us for his glory, but he also saves us for his glory (Rom. 9:22–23). And then he bestows the grace-giving power of speech on each of us, that we might each be "the other's inspiration." But we must ask again, "What does grace-giving speech look like?"

> Mercy withholds punishment deserved.
> Grace gives holy gifts from God's reserve.

Grace is *giving*. Grace offers a way up and out from the darkness. It pulls people from where they are to the place God's love wants them to be. That can happen in a host of ways. It could mean pulling someone out of self-deprecation and into God-honoring self-worth. It could mean drawing someone away from being critical of others. It could mean asking an open-ended question and listening—just listening—to someone's experience in the world. But how is all this related to God's

---

2. Malcolm Guite, "Trinity Sunday" in *Sounding the Seasons: Seventy Sonnets for the Christian Year* (London: Canterbury, 2012), 48.

presence? Well, grace is the door to God's personal presence. Eternal communion with him is only available through grace. Words that give grace to others usher them into the presence of God, the one who both knows and loves them completely. When our words give grace to others, they also turn shoulders towards the God who gave his Son that they might live in him.

In sum, when we push away the falsehood of the great lie and embrace the truth of God's presence, our words can build up others, fit the occasion, and give grace to those who hear. Each of those effects is closely tied to God's presence—the one who provides worth, self-sacrificing love, and grace for his image bearers.

In words the world was broken. But in words, it will be remade.

When our words tear others down, push them away from God's loving presence, and suggest that God's grace does not include them, that's when we speak damaging words linked to the great lie of God's absence. In the context of the great lie, God's authoritative presence is not here to call for building up. The "fit occasion" becomes whatever serves us best at the time, and grace-giving turns to selfish opportunism. We see this all over the place in our world. I don't need to offer examples. And rather than looking at what other people are doing, it's more productive to focus on what *we're* doing with our words. How are they affecting people?

God is calling us to honor his presence with words that point others to him. In words the world was broken. But in words, it will be remade.

Reflection Questions and Prayer

1. What are some damaging words someone has spoken to you? How did they affect you?
2. What are some Ephesians 4:29 words that someone has spoken to you? How did they affect you?
3. Take one conversation from your week and write down a "Paradise Perspective" on them. What do you notice?
4. Pull out one sentence you speak or write this week. What does that sentence say about God's presence?

Prayer

God, the great lie has led us to speak damaging words,
Words that don't point others to your presence.
Our words tear down and promote self.
They push others away from you.
In the Spirit, we know you change us.
You call us to participate in redemption,
To speak words that give grace to those who hear.
Help us to cultivate grace-giving speech,
To turn the shoulders of listeners
To your great and gracious presence.

9
OUR ACTIONS AND GOD'S PRESENCE

We've now seen how the great lie affects our thoughts and our words. By God's grace, we can think and speak in a way that honors his presence and draws others to him. But thoughts and words often mature into actions. What might it look like to act in honor of God's presence, to counter the great lie in the little things we do each day?

Growth and Change

At heart, we're talking about how people grow and change, how their yesterday-self is different from their today-self, how godly thoughts and words make an impact on their behavior. Theologians call this *sanctification*, the process of God's Spirit conforming us more to the image of God's Son. We need to get a sense of how that happens more generally before we dive into a discussion of how we can act in faithful witness to God's presence.

David Powlison (1949–2019) was a gentle sage who left the world earlier than we thought he would. His little book *How Does Sanctification Work?* is a wonderful gift to us.[1] He doesn't present an exact method to follow regarding how we grow and

---

1. David Powlison, *How Does Sanctification Work?* (Wheaton, IL: Crossway, 2017).

change, which is probably what most people want. But life doesn't often fit neatly into methods. What he does provide is a way of understanding the avenues through which change can come, calling us to see how multiple avenues are often being used simultaneously. What are these avenues? *God, truth, people, suffering,* and *your own heart.*[2] But all of these work in us because we encounter the presence of God in Jesus Christ. He writes, "When Jesus crosses paths with you, he reveals you for who you are. He precipitates decisive choices. In response to him, people change, either making a turn for the better or taking a turn for the worse."[3] We change and grow because the presence of God confronts us in Christ.

Let's look at each of these avenues in the context of the great lie and how we might honor God's presence in response.

We change and grow because the presence of God confronts us in Christ.

God. The wild God of hemlocks and herons, ocean swells and dust storms, who speaks to ravens and makes the stones sing—he breaks through to you. He "intervenes in your life, turning you from suicidal self-will to the kingdom of life. He raises you in Christ when you are dead in trespasses and sins. He restores hearing when you are deaf (you could not hear him otherwise). He gives sight when you are blind (you could not see

---

2. Powlison, *How Does Sanctification Work?*, 63.

3. Powlison, *How Does Sanctification Work?*, 13.

him otherwise). He is immediately and personally present, a life-creating voice, a strong and strengthening hand."[4] Personally present—God changes you simply by *being here*. And he acts.

The great lie whispers the opposite: that God *isn't* here and that he *can't* or *won't* change you. Don't we feel like that sometimes? Over the past week, I heard two songs from the same artist on the radio, both of which said something about how the singer "can't change" even if he tried. Though I disagreed based on what I know of the power of God, I understood the sentiment. Many people feel trapped in a cold world, as if their patterns of behavior have hardened into ice, and no one can break the winter.

God breaks winter to bring spring. He breaks death to bring life.

But God always breaks the winter. He breaks night to bring day. He breaks winter to bring spring. He breaks death to bring life. God is in the business of changing what we think must go on forever. It takes a lot of faith to believe that, spread over years and decades. But that's what God's word calls us to grip in hope. He is present with us and is going to change us. He's going to raise up the good seed he's sown in us by the Spirit (Phil. 1:6). How exactly will he do this? It will likely involve combinations of the other avenues. To make this concrete, I'll use an example from my own life. I want to have a consuming

---

4. Powlison, *How Does Sanctification Work?*, 64.

desire for God and not for the things the world offers that often tempt me—namely money, success, and attention from others. So I ask the God who is present to change me. And I'll ask him again, right now. "God, capture my heart with your beauty, your glory, your compassion, and your self-giving. May my greatest longing be for you."

Truth. The avenue of truth comes to us via Scripture. "Scripture speaks with a true voice into a world churning with false voices. Scripture reveals innumerable features of God's person, purposes, will, promises, and actions. Scripture clarifies every facet of human experience. I come to know myself truly as I live before the eyes of the One whose opinion matters."[5] Truth is the soul's true north, and it comes from the mouth of God (Deut. 8:3).

What Powlison points out here is something we often ignore: *we're always listening to voices.* It's not a matter of *whether* we're listening to some voice in our daily life; it's a matter of *which voice.* We assume our days are filled with decisions we make on our own. But every decision—from how you cook your breakfast to what you text your friend—travels within the sound waves of a voice. It could be the voice of God and his self-sacrificing love, the voice of the Spirit. It could be the voice of selfishness. It could be the voice of material comfort. All our decisions happen within the soundwaves of some voice. Nothing we do is done in a vacuum. Our actions reverberate in the context of larger vibrations, broader voices, whether true or false.

---

5. Powlison, *How Does Sanctification Work?*, 64.

The great lie is one of those false voices Powlison mentions—one of the most devastating. It's the voice of Satan himself, the father of lies. Satan's voice always tells us to be *like* God instead of being *with* God.[6] He wants us to act in rebellion against God's authoritative presence, to act *as if* God isn't always with us, to act *as if* we're autonomous. We've already seen how Scripture addresses the great lie with testaments to God's great presence. Psalm 139:7–12 is perhaps one of the most well known. And if we're craving something even more concrete, we have Jesus's great promise in Matthew 28:20. "I am with you always, to the end of the age." If you believe in Christ, then by the power of the Spirit Jesus Christ is *with* you. Right now.

How does this influence my longing to change, to have a consuming desire for God and not for money, success, and attention from others? I know that God will be faithful to change me, since I've asked him to do what he's already promised to do: to complete the good work he's started in me. But now I can rest on the truth of his word as a guide. In fact, one of the passages he's drawn me back to today is 2 Corinthians 6:8–10.

> We are treated as impostors, and yet are true; [9] as unknown, and yet well known; as dying, and behold, we live; as punished, and yet not killed; [10] as sorrowful, yet always rejoicing; as poor, yet making many rich; as having nothing, yet possessing everything.

---

6. Chris Nye, *Distant God: Why He Feels Far Away and What We Can Do about It* (Chicago: Moody, 2016), chap. 2. Kindle edition.

"Everything." That seems to encompass much *more* than money, success, and attention from others. In Christ, I already have everything. I just don't see it in the way my little mind envisions. I don't have an extra home in the Swiss Alps or an intimidating stock portfolio. I haven't won the Pulitzer or landed on the New York Times Bestseller list. And I don't have swaths of people telling me how great I am. But all of that is *small*. In the context of what *God* has done in giving *himself* for billions of souls at enmity with him, what I long for is petty. God raised the dead and set up rooms for his beloved in a breathtaking mansion, in a country that's too beautiful for words, not because of what it looks like but because of *his own presence*. God is far greater than I can imagine, and his presence offers riches no one can count. Jesus, the resurrected Lord, the Son of God in the flesh, is in the room with me right now. He's *here*, and he's never leaving. My longing for material and earthly things pales in comparison to my longing for the one who made all of that, but who offers me much more: himself. The problem with my heart is that I still struggle to see how *he* is more valuable than *things*. But little by little, his word teaches me. God's speech turns my shoulders away from the shimmering things of the world and towards the light of his own presence. His word is changing me.

People. So, God changes me, and his word also changes me. But other people play a part in my changing, too. "Godly growth is most frequently mediated through the gifts and graces of brothers and sisters in Christ."[7] When the great lie asserts that

---

7. Powlison, *How Does Sanctification Work?*, 65.

God isn't present, that also means that he isn't present through mediaries, through his image bearers. God's spoken presence always comes to us through means—through creation, through his word, through the prophets, through Christ, through the apostles, and through God's people. When people steeped in the wisdom of God's Spirit engage with us, they mediate God's presence to us, and it changes us.

Again, how does this change me in my desire to long for God alone, and not for things of the world? Well, I know of one brother in the Lord blessed with money, and do you know what he does with it? *He gives it away.* His giving is constant and generous—jaw-droppingly generous. And that helps me understand something: *money doesn't deliver on its promise to fulfill us.* I know that already, of course. But my heart pushes back against that when financial struggles come my way. I believe the lie that money is what will resolve the tension, and not the God who grants prosperity in his own way. When I see someone giving so much away, it changes my heart. It tells me, "Money isn't the answer that you think it is. Go back to God." I know another brother in Christ who epitomizes professional success as a writer, churning out books left and right, and truly embodying the biblical wisdom he writes about. His response to all of this: *it's not important.* I think, "What?! Well, of course it's important! Don't you see how many people you're influencing?" It's not important because it's not *his* name he's trying to establish in the world; it's *Christ's*. Worldly success says, "Make a name for yourself." Wise people say, "How can I elevate the name of Christ?" There's a big difference. The former will be more recognizable by others. The latter will often go unseen. The former will get the world's attention. The latter will get God's attention, who sees in secret and measures the motives of the heart. The more I surround myself with wise people in the Lord, the more I'll be changed by them.

Suffering. God, his truth, and wise people change us, but so do hard things. That was my main motive for writing *Finding Hope in Hard Things*. Hard things change us in ways easy things don't. Powlison testifies to the same truth.

> God works on us in the midst of trouble because trouble catches our attention. Difficulties make us need him. Faith has to sink roots, as profession deepens into reality. . . . . The difficulties that we experience necessitate grace by awakening a true sense of weakness and need. This is where the Spirit is working. People change because something is hard, not because everything goes well.[8]

The experiences that have changed me most have been the most crushing. Over time, I've been amazed to see how much the Spirit works on my soul in those experiences. Watching my father die in front of me from cancer when I was eighteen.[9] Battling a crippling anxiety disorder for over fifteen years.[10] Wrestling with self-doubt that constantly calls me to quit. These things are tough. But they've also changed me in far

---

8. Powlison, *How Does Sanctification Work?*, 66.

9. *I Am a Human: A Memoir on Grief, Identity, and Hope.*

10. *Struck Down but Not Destroyed: Living Faithfully with Anxiety.*

greater ways than any success or comfort has.

Of course, these are the places where the great lie can be the most destructive. How easy it was to think that God wasn't with me when I was in the pits of grief over my father! And how natural it is to think that God is absent when you're in the middle of a panic attack! These are situations when our *feelings* pulse like a drum beat, calling us away from the truth we know. But they can also be times when we are closest to the Lord, as we share in his suffering (Phil. 3:10; 2 Cor. 1:5). They can be times when the presence of God is most accessible to us. And they're certainly helpful in reminding us of what matters most: our closeness and communion with God. Suffering shows me that—more than money or success or the approval of others—what I really want is God. Suffering changes me by burning away the fog of lesser desires.

Suffering changes me by burning away the fog of lesser desires.

Your own heart. Lastly, we can be changed in our own heart, fully active in taking a new direction. Here's Powlison again:

We turn—from darkness to light, from false gods to the only true God, from death to life, from unbelief to faith. You ask for help because you need help. You repent. You believe, trust, seek, take refuge. You are honest. You remember, listen, obey, fear, hope, love, give thanks, weep, confess, praise, delight, walk. Notice all these active verbs; they speak of wholehearted, whole-person action. These are the fruitful characteristics of a flourishing life. No one does any of this for you. You are not passive. You are not a puppet or a robot. You are 100 percent responsible, and yet you are 100 percent dependent on outside help.[11]

I love that last line; it's the epitome of the gospel. We make a choice, and yet we're wholly dependent on God to save. The same applies to how we change. We act, but we always need God.

The great lie enters here to try and trick us into the "bootstrapping approach" to life. Satan says, "See! You're changing all on your own. You don't need God for this. He's not even here, anyway. This is all you!" Like Adam and Eve, we can be tempted to perceive our action as "all our own," without having any implications for a divine-human relationship. If God were absent, then Adam and Eve's decision would have no relevance for their relationship with him. But he's always present. Their decision affected their relationship with God. And the same applies to our decisions. We don't act in isolation. Every act we take occurs within the arena of God's presence, and it has an impact on our relationship with God. The great lie suggests that our actions are wholly independent. But our hearts know better, and so do our heads. Everything God has made, remember, reveals his presence to us. Deep in the caverns of our hearts, we know he's present. And life is a network of choices emanating from our hearts.

---

11. Powlison, *How Does Sanctification Work?*, 67.

Once more, this maps onto my prayer that God would change me and give me a desire only for him. This is a heart request. I know that my heart is at war. Though I've been won by Christ, Satan won't put his weapons down. He keeps taking jabs at me. He keeps suggesting God is absent and that my heart is adrift in a world that's cold and lonely. But in his mysterious ways, God works in my heart, pushing me towards him. I act, and yet I'm wholly dependent on him. I only turn towards him because his extended hand is there to pull me closer.

Growth in Acting for Others

All of the avenues for change we discussed above are related to a deeper change in us, a turn away from self and towards others. God is self-giving. His presence is given to us in Christ and by the Spirit. Our actions honor God's presence by putting others' needs above our own. B. B. Warfield has a beautiful statement about this, and it's a fitting end to this chapter. I know it is because it was a fitting end to Powlison's book, too.

> Christ was led by His love for others, into the world, to forget Himself in the needs of others, to sacrifice self once for all upon the altar of sympathy. Self-sacrifice brought Christ into the world. And self-sacrifice will lead us, His followers, not away from but into the midst of men.[12]

"Perhaps," Powlison writes, "the most dramatic evidence of

12. B. B. Warfield, "Imitating the Incarnation," in *The Person and Work of Christ*, ed. Samuel Craig (Philadelphia: Presbyterian and Reformed, 1950), 574–575.

headway in sanctification is that you no longer think so much about yourself."[13]   Our real test as to whether our actions are honoring God's presence or not is simple: *Are you doing something for yourself, or are you really doing it for someone else?* God-honoring actions are always those that place the other above the self. Whenever we act this way, we assault the great lie by affirming the presence of the self-giving God.

Reflection Questions and Prayer

1. What actions of other people have had the most impact on you? Why?
2. What difficulties do you have in either measuring or perceiving change in your own spiritual life?
3. Think of a recent act you committed that was influenced by the great lie. How did it affect your soul? How did it affect others?
4. What is an act you can do today that would affirm the presence of the self-giving God?

Prayer

God, we long to change.
We long to act in self-giving love.
But we confess that we're preoccupied.
We serve ourselves before we serve others.
We focus on what we *get* from Christ,

---

13. Powlison, *How Does Sanctification Work?*, 66.

Not on what we can *give* to him.
We need your help to honor your presence,
To assault the great lie.
We know you are always with us,
And we want you to change us
So that we always long to be with you,
Above all else.
Change us yourself,
Through your word,
By your people,
In hard things,
In our hearts.
Help us to act out a self-giving life.

10
GOD'S ANSWER TO THE GREAT LIE

T ruth be told, I've been writing the whole book just so
I could get to this chapter. I've alluded to the truth
this chapter will unpack in the previous ones. But
now it's time to stare, marvel, and worship.

What is God's answer to the great lie, to the claim that he
isn't really present with us? His answer—think of how wild this
is!—is not a proposition. It is a *person*. He didn't argue with
many words to convince us; he argued with the Word for us.
Christ is God's great answer to the great lie. In this chapter, let's
unpack all that means for us. But not without a bit of marveling
first. Poetry always helps me to marvel, so I'll offer these lines.

He Said

A silent God would never do,
Not for Adam, and not for Eve.
We needed to be told what's true.
Only his words could bring reprieve.

And so God gave them—means to mirth.
Our life was tied to syllables.
God uttered, and we felt our worth;
His speech made us forgivable.

He spoke to tell us he was here,
Amidst the trees, behind the sun.
And into every listening ear
He gave his word: he'd never run.

He would stay close, always present,
Though we would cling to the great lie
That no king resides with peasants,
No God could live where men would die.

Still he continued, whispering strong;
Even called out bodies from the grave.
But we didn't listen very long.
We'd need a greater Word to save.

And so God gave *him*, Son of man,
The Lord of heaven wrapped in earth,
Light of light, the heart of his plan
To give us all a second birth.

God's presence spoken into flesh
To wave and walk and carry on,
A stalk of wheat that we would thresh,
A presence men would prey upon.

And so they preyed, and off he went,
Right into Joseph's rocky tomb.

There in the dark God's presence lay,
Wound in cloth and our own perfume.

But

A silent Word would never do,
Not for Pilate, and not for Paul.
Through death the Word was uttered new,
Resurrected speech for us all.

So do not ask for God to speak.
He's done that in our doubt and dread.
He speaks his presence to the weak.
We are alive because he said.

Exchanging the Lie for the Truth

If the great lie is that God isn't really present with us, then we start to see just how beautiful Jesus's title is: *Immanuel*, the with-us God. The great answer to the great lie is the great presence of the great God. And this has everything to do with us moving from the great lie into the great truth.

In a previous chapter, we talked about lies as *deceiving mental maps*. They tell us to go where we shouldn't go. They trick us into thinking that something false is true. Lies tell us how *not* to live. They balk at the presence of God. Truth calls us back to that presence in humility.

We miss this connection between truth and God's presence, don't we? Vern Poythress helps us find it again. He ties truth to trust and heart.[1]

> The fundamental issue at the level of the heart is whether
> we love God or not (Deut. 6:5). Do we trust, then, that what
> he says is true and is for our good? Or do we listen to the
> serpent, who insinuates that God is withholding something
> that would be good for us? The test for Adam is whether he
> will listen to the truth, the truth of God, or to falsehood, the
> falsehood of the devil. The truth leads to life. The way of
> falsehood leads to death.[2]

Slow down and process this. Falsehood leads to death.
Truth leads to life. In our context, the falsehood is the great lie,
that God isn't authoritatively present. That leads not merely to
difficulty or frustration but to *death*. The result of fully believing
in the great lie is the expiration of the soul. And when we
partially or intermittently believe it, we can feel our spirit wane.
Remember, lies take us somewhere. They aren't just a game in
intellectual trickery. They are maps that lead us to dangerous
places, and eventually to death.

On the other side is the truth of God. But this truth is not
simply a proposition. It's not an abstract concept, though our
minds have been schooled to think of truth that way. In the
biblical sense, truth is bound up with the personhood of God.
That's why Jesus says not "I speak the truth" but "I *am* the

---

1. For a bit more on this, see "Truth Asks for Trust," Westminster Magazine,
https://wm.wts.edu/content/truth-asks-for-trust.

2. Vern S. Poythress, *Truth, Theology, and Perspective: An Approach to Understanding Biblical Doctrine* (Wheaton, IL: Crossway, 2022), 85.

truth" (John 14:6). This expression should puzzle us. We assume lies and truth are only dealing with information. But God says they're dealing with *him*. When we embrace the truth of the gospel, we embrace the truth of who God is, not only what he's done. Believing in the truth leads not merely to intellectual accuracy but personal indwelling. "If anyone loves me, he will keep my word, and my Father will love him, and we will come to him and make our home with him" (John 14:23). "Do you not know that your body is a temple of the Holy Spirit within you, whom you have from God? You are not your own" (1 Cor. 6:19). Believing the truth doesn't just mean you've "got it right." It means you're indwelt by the three persons of the Godhead!

Believing in the truth leads not merely to intellectual accuracy but personal indwelling.

Now, we have a shameful history of exchanging the truth for a lie (Rom. 1:25), of replacing the God of truth with the falsehood of Satan. And that leads to some horrible things. Do you know what happens when we exchange the truth of God's presence in Christ for the lie of his absence? Paul has a list for us.

> [28] And since they did not see fit to acknowledge God, God gave them up to a debased mind to do what ought not to be done. [29] They were filled with all manner of unrighteousness,

evil, covetousness, malice. They are full of envy, murder, strife, deceit, maliciousness. They are gossips, [30] slanderers, haters of God, insolent, haughty, boastful, inventors of evil, disobedient to parents, [31] foolish, faithless, heartless, ruthless. [32] Though they know God's righteous decree that those who practice such things deserve to die, they not only do them but give approval to those who practice them. (Rom. 1:28–32)

Well . . . gee. That's a pretty horrendous list. Turns out that embracing a lie gets you into a lot more trouble than mental dissonance. If lies take us somewhere, then *this* is the destination—a whole string of cringeworthy maladies ending in death.

That's why the truth of God's embodied presence in Christ is such good news. Embracing the personal presence of God, embracing the truth, doesn't just make us intellectually correct. It leads to rebirth, to an entirely different way of living.

Let's break this down in the context of John's Gospel. Have you ever wondered what Jesus meant in John 3:5–6? "Truly, truly, I say to you, unless one is born of water and the Spirit, he cannot enter the kingdom of God. That which is born of the flesh is flesh, and that which is born of the Spirit is spirit." Later in John's Gospel he says that *he* is the only way to enter the kingdom of God his Father. "I am the way, and the truth, and the life. No one comes to the Father except through me." So, to enter the kingdom, you need to be born of water and the Spirit through Christ.

The problem is that people are naturally born "of the flesh."

Paul later calls this being born "of dust" (1 Cor. 15:47). The only way to enter the kingdom of God, then, is to walk *through* the door of Christ (John 10:7, 9). Upon entering into faith in *him*, we go through a second birth, a birth "of water and the Spirit." Water, used in the Old Testament laws for cleansing and in the New Testament for baptism, symbolizes purification, a washing away of filth and sin. The resulting purity makes us children of the Spirit of God. And that's something John introduced in the first chapter of his Gospel. "But to all who did receive him, who believed in his name, he gave the right to become children of God, who were born, not of blood nor of the will of the flesh nor of the will of man, but of God" (John 1:12–13). And yet, notice this: the Spirit of God is also the Spirit of truth (John 16:13). Do you see how all the lines of God's trinitarian work are intersecting, and how it's all bound up with truth and life? As children of the dust, we need to enter *through* the truth (the person of Christ) in order to be purified *by* the Spirit of truth (the person of the Spirit) so that we can have fellowship *with* the God of truth, the one who is going to crush Satan (Rom. 16:20)—the great liar. The great lie is going to be crushed by the great triune God of truth!

Embracing the great truth of God's presence in Christ and casting out the great lie of his absence means gaining a new life, a higher life, an *eternal* life. We've exchanged the truth of God for a lie long enough. It's time to exchange the lie of Satan for the truth of God, and to do it everyday by affirming, "God. Is. Here."

All of this helps us to take a step further and answer the

questions, "What does it mean to enjoy God's personal presence?" And "What does our eternal destiny look like in God's presence?"

Presence in a Person

To enjoy God's presence in a person is quite mysterious. But isn't this what we've always wanted? Isn't it what we still want? We took time in earlier chapters to note that God is an invisible Spirit, and we can't sense him in the way we would sense created persons. Instead, we perceive his *spoken presence* in creation and in Scripture. Yet, the great truth that confronts the great lie is the glorious coming of Jesus Christ, the eternal Speech of God who put on clothing and walked among us. Jesus was God's speech in visible form. Those who lived during his time on earth *actually witnessed* the embodied presence of God.

We might be tempted to envy those people, as if we drew the short straw in being born after the time of Christ. Why don't *we* get to enjoy God's manifested presence in Jesus? Why don't we get to touch him, hear him, stare at him?

Note two things here. First, most of God's people are in the exact same position that we are. They either looked forward to God's incarnate presence or else looked back on that presence after Christ's ascension. Living during the time of Christ was a rarity, and God has purposes for that. Conversely, he must have very good purposes for us *not* being able to see Christ for those thirty-three years he was on earth.

Second, Jesus Christ himself said that it was *good* for him to go away. "I tell you the truth: it is to your advantage that I go away, for if I do not go away, the Helper will not come to you. But if I go, I will send him to you" (John 16:7). It's to our *advantage* for Christ not to be here right now. It's to our *advantage* that the incarnate presence of God has now ascended. Why? Because now we have the Spirit. And the Spirit is our soul's leader, the one who will guide us into all truth (John 16:13), which is going deeper into Jesus himself! Jesus is saying that, somehow, it's to our advantage that his glorious, incarnate presence, the great answer to the great lie, has ascended to the right hand of God. And the key reason he gives is that this is what triggers the sending of the Spirit.

During the time of Christ, his people enjoyed his presence on the outside. Christ was a person in front of them, around them, behind them. But he was always on the outside. While we might yearn for communion with that external presence of God, Jesus sends the Spirit so that we might have him *inside* of us through the Spirit. And that's much deeper communion, isn't it? We've always wanted a way *into* deep fellowship with God, a way *into* the peace of his presence. This draws to mind one of C. S. Lewis's statements about what we're all after: the beauty of God's presence.

> We do not want merely to see beauty, though, God knows, even that is bounty enough. We want something else which can hardly be put into words—to be united with the beauty we see, to pass into it, to receive it into ourselves, to bathe in it, to become part of it ... At present we are on the outside of the world, the wrong side of the door. We discern the

freshness and purity of morning, but they do not make us fresh and pure. We cannot mingle with the splendours we see. But all the leaves of the New Testament are rustling with the rumour that it will not always be so. Some day, God willing, we shall get in.[3]

We want a way *in*. That's the Holy Ghost. We have the personal presence of God inside us through the Spirit. The God of all the beauty that radiates through the world and makes us long for eternity—who whispers out the cirrus clouds and beckons the breakers, who redeems the sordid blood of sinners by birthing himself into it—that God now lives *inside* us.

Haunted by the Holy Ghost

I've always loved the title "Holy Ghost" for the third person of the Trinity. I hadn't realized why until the moment of my writing this. Much of the time, our souls feel like ghost barns. See, when a barn gets decrepit and falls into disrepair, farmers could tear it down. But that usually costs more time and labor than seems worth it. So, they let old barns stand in the fields and by the roadside; they let the wood gray and weather. They leave the structure to the elements until all that's left is a ghost of use, a storehouse for swallows, a memory of hooves and horses. That's how Satan leaves us, isn't it? The great liar is finished with us once he believes he's destroyed our use for the

---

3. C. S. Lewis, *The Weight of Glory* (repr., New York: HarperOne, 2001), 42–43, quoted in Chris Nye, *Distant God: Why He Feels Far Away and What We Can Do about It* (Chicago: Moody, 2016), chap. 13. Kindle edition

Lord. He's happy to let us decompose in the sun and rain, to be an emblem of loss and missed opportunity.

But then the Holy Ghost shows up in the wind, comes to haunt us, fills us with a hope we can't see. He takes what's dead and makes it live. He lets the birds stay, but he sures up the rafters and pulls the boards tighter. We can feel ourselves strong again. We become, after much work, a home for others, a place for travelers to rest, even for humble animals. We become, in other words, a place of *giving*, a building that resembles the prodigal God.

I want to be haunted. And so do you. We long to be filled with God, to enter into him and have him enter into us, never to leave. That's what we have in the Spirit, in our Holy Ghost. Jesus left so that we could be haunted by God.

The Haunting

I was a barn for God, broken, gray, and tired.
The horses and the hounds all left;
The owls and the swallows rest
Their hollow bones on hay bale nests.
It seems my spirit has transpired.

The devil came as a farmer black.
He sent the animals away
And told no travelers to stay.
I couldn't keep the rain at bay,
And all I have is lack.

Then came a holy bird in me.
He perched upon my weakest beam,
Told me it was time to dream
Of horse and hen and hay bale steam,
Of housing life resiliently.

"And as you shelter, never boast,"
He said from on the rafter.
"When you are strong hereafter,
And trade sorrow for laughter,
Rehearse what matters most."

"You are no place for vaunting."
My tired frame just nodded,
As the old bird hopped and plodded,
Singing of the home he spotted:
"I am here for haunting."

So, we have the personal presence of God in the Spirit, the holy haunter, a way to enter *into* the beauty and love and labors of God. But we also have God's *eternal presence* to wage war against the great threat against humanity: death itself.

Eternal Presence

Death has always haunted me. I came to the faith as a shaking, silent seven-year-old, creeping into the dark of a hotel room to ask my father what I had to do to avoid death and get to heaven.

The fear that night shaped me, molded my mind and found its way into my muscles. It drew me into asking *the question*, which was my salvation. So, great good came from heavy fear that night.

Years later, at 18, as I stared down at my father's limp and decaying body, shaking and silent again at the threat of death taking away the shepherding giant of my life, I wept. Death had come to ravage me and my hero. I'd nearly forgotten about death, lived many years without acknowledging his presence in every room. But no more. I had what counselors tell me was a PTSD response to his passing that June evening, which rolled into a full-blown anxiety disorder that's followed me around for fifteen years.

Death comes back regularly—when leukemia claims your dear grandmother, when spinal cancer comes for your friend at 31, when a car crash claims that basketball teammate you were never that close to, when pancreatic tumors steal away a sage in the faith and threaten a new friend with an early end. Oh, death . . .

My nerves get the better of me when death comes. Almost immediately my heart starts moving faster, sensing the threat like a wild animal. Hypervigilance takes over. I feel out of control, and then I feel embarrassed and ashamed for feeling out of control. Isn't my faith stronger than this? Shouldn't I be able to stare death in the face and smile? Why am I still so fearful? What should I do?

We know those bold and brilliant verses from Paul:

When the perishable puts on the imperishable, and the mortal puts on immortality, then shall come to pass the saying that is written:

"Death is swallowed up in victory."

"O death, where is your victory?

O death, where is your sting?" (1 Cor. 15:54–55)

I haven't put on the imperishable yet. That's the problem. I have faith that death is swallowed up in victory. I have faith that its sting has vanished. But what do we do when the ghost of death is still haunting us?

We stare at an eternity of God's good and glorious presence. When we stare at what's right in front of us, the world can seem to fracture and fall apart. We lose heart. Faith slips through our fingers. We despair. But when we stare at what's ahead of us, fixing our eyes on that holy horizon of eternity with God, we anticipate. We dream. We hope for what's coming. And we remember something that's so easy to forget when death is haunting us: we are immortal in the great truth, in Jesus Christ, in the one who burst through the doors of death. Say it slowly. Own the words. *I. Am. Immortal.* That ridiculous claim is the clear implication of Jesus's words: "I am the resurrection and the life. Whoever believes in me, though he die, yet shall he live, and everyone who lives and believes in me shall never die" (John 11:25–26). "Never die." That's immortality. If you and I believe in Jesus Christ, God's great answer to Satan's great lie, we are immortal.

That immortality is pointing right into the gates of eternity.

That's our destination. That's what lies before us—not cancer or heart trouble or alheizmers. Those things just get in the way. Our destination can't even be thwarted by death or by our own paralyzing fear of it. Eternity is coming for us, not just death. We are immortal.

If you and I believe in Jesus Christ, God's great answer to Satan's great lie, we are immortal.

But immortality alone isn't enough, strange as that sounds. We will be immortal with the God of glory. In C. S. Lewis's words, we will be *in* with the God of beauty. And there will be no end to the communion. Immortality is only meaningful if God is immanent, if he'll be there with us. And he will be. Our heavenly Father is preparing rooms for us right now, like a holy hotel concierge.

Let not your hearts be troubled. Believe in God; believe also in me. ² In my Father's house are many rooms. If it were not so, would I have told you that I go to prepare a place for you? ³ And if I go and prepare a place for you, I will come again and will take you to myself, that where I am you may be also. ⁴ And you know the way to where I am going. (John 14:1–4)

Jesus, of course, *is* the way, just as he is the truth. He is the answer to the great lie. He is the one whom we will dwell with, along with the Father and the Spirit. I love the words "that where I am you may be also." I want to be with him. I want to sit at his feet—with my father, and grandmother, and a multitude of my brothers and sisters from across time and space—and hear him speak. I want to embrace him. I want to be where he is. And that's heaven. Heaven is the place where Satan's great lie is laughed at.

Until that day, the grief and fear and doubt we deal with when death haunts us is troubling because it's blinding. It gets in the way of our clear vision of eternity. It calls us to question our immortality. But we can see past the ghost of death. In fact, if we're staring at eternity, we can see right *through* him. When we keep eternity in focus, Satan and his lies are nothing more than a mist.

I was always told not to stare as a child. Like all advice, it only applies to certain contexts. Staring is the best advice we can give others and ourselves in the context of death. Stare at Christ in his resurrected glory. Stare at the Spirit's ongoing support of your tired soul. Stare at the gates of eternity and point: "There. There. There. That's where I'm going. Christ, you made me immortal." I need to get better at staring, especially when death, an offshoot of the great lie, threatens my heart. May the words below be true for us all.

Death can haunt and jab and shove.
It can bind your heart and blind your eyes.
It belittles hope and joy and love.
It pulls your vision from the skys.

But Christ broke through the dark of death.
He calls us in and lifts our chins,
So we can live within his rest
And stare at gates where life begins.

Reflection Questions and Prayer

1. In what ways is Christ God's answer to the great lie?
2. How do we cultivate deeper communion with God through the Holy Spirit?
3. Think of the last time you had to face death. What was your response? How does staring at eternity with God affect your response?
4. If we're meant to stare at an eternity with God, how does that affect our daily approach to life?

Prayer

God of presence and eternal peace,
You spoke out against the great lie.
You came to us in a person, in your Son.
You showed yourself among us,
And then you gave yourself for us.
And after Christ ascended,
You gave yourself to us again in the Spirit.
You are such a prodigal God!
Help us to stare at you when death threatens us.
Help us to know that in Christ we are immortal.
Show us how to stare at an eternity with you.

And when our hearts doubt,
Give us the faith we need to fight our unbelief.

II

LIVING IN THE SPIRIT OF TRUTH

S o, here we are. You and I have been given God's answer
to the great lie: the person of truth. That person has
told us he is always present with us (Matt. 28:20). We've
been given Christ, and we've also been given the Holy Spirit,
Christ's Spirit (Rom. 8:11), the Spirit of truth (John 14:17).
Given these amazing realities, how are we supposed to live?
How do we live in the Spirit of truth? And what does it look
like when the great lie is still peeking at us from around every
corner?

Living in Response

When God speaks, things happen. God's speech always *affects*
those it addresses. The pattern for this is set out in creation,
when the Trinity has a holy conversation that results in . . . well,
everything. The Father spoke the Son, and the Spirit carried
that speech into tangible results. Poythress notes,

> In each act of creation, we can see three phases. There is the
> plan, which is always there. Then there is the going out of the
> truth. This going out is a communication. God speaks. And
> then there is the obedience that responds to the command.[1]

---

1. Vern S. Poythress, *Truth, Theology, and Perspective: An Approach to Understanding Biblical Doctrine* (Wheaton, IL: Crossway, 2022), 54,

He goes on. Pay close attention to the end of the following quotation.

> The archetype of communication of the truth is found in God himself. . . . The Father is the speaker; the Son is the Word; and the Holy Spirit functions as the breath bringing the word to its destination. This pattern is reflected when God speaks in order to create the world. God the Father is preeminently the speaker. It is implied that he has a plan to speak, even before he speaks. The Word, the second person of the Trinity, is expressed in the speech ("Let there be light," Gen. 1:3). The Holy Spirit is present, "hovering over the face of the waters" (Gen. 1:2). His immediate presence results in effects in the world. The word that God sends out is impressed on the things in the world.[2]

What happens when the Father utters the Word of truth? The Spirit is present to produce *effects* in the world. Just as creation responded to the creative word of God in Genesis, we all respond to the saving Word of truth that God has given in Jesus Christ. Our response is the work of God's own Spirit. So, what does it look like to live in the Spirit of truth? It looks like we are *responding* to the truth.

The truth, Jesus Christ and his Spirit, is God's redemptive presence with us—the one who forgives our sins and makes us more and more like the Son, more *true*, more like God. Of

---

2. Poythress, *Truth, Theology, and Perspective*, 55.

course, we can respond to the truth in lots of ways, depending on our context. Let's look at some of these ways so that we can have options for measuring our own response to God's Word of truth.

Ways of Responding

We've already talked about changing and growing in acting for others. Certainly, that's a central part of what it means to respond to the Spirit of truth. God uses the five avenues we explored in a previous chapter to enact change in us, to help us respond to himself: God, his word, other people, suffering, and our own hearts. It would help to spend a bit more time on the difficult areas in the remainder of this chapter, focusing on how the Spirit of truth works to destroy the effects of the great lie in us.

Accepting suffering as a teacher. This area aligns with Powlison's discussion of "suffering" as a means for change. But it's likely the hardest thing for us to accept. Dane Ortlund uses a gardening illustration (as Scripture itself does) to portray it.

Each of us is like an otherwise healthy vine that has the perverse inclination to entangle all its tendrils around a poisonous tree that appears nourishing but actually deadens us. We have been warned that embracing this tree will kill us. But we can't help ourselves. We wrap ourselves around it. There's only one resort for the loving gardener. He must slice us free. Lop off whole branches, even. He must cause us to pass through the pass of loss, the pain of being diminished, of being lessened, in order to free us.

The world and its fraudulent offerings are like that poisonous tree. And our heavenly Gardener loves us too much to let us continue to commit soul suicide by getting more and more deeply attached to the world. Through the pain of disappointment and frustration, God weans us from the love of this world. It feels like we're being crippled, like we're dying. In point of fact, we are being freed from the counterfeit pleasures of the world.[3]

No one wants to feel the sting of pain, the bitterness of loss or frustration. But the taste of suffering doesn't reflect its purpose.

Still, this nasty taste of suffering draws out an instinctive repulsion. We feel as if this is *wrong*, whatever "this" is. We think suffering is an alien invasion, an anomaly. But if we entered the current world *through* pain via sin, doesn't it make sense that we'd have to go back *out* of the world through it, that just as suffering was a road *to* Satan's kingdom, it would also be the road *out of* it? God doesn't always make new roads; he redeems old ones. He turns Satan's wishes against him. While the world is surely broken by sin, that doesn't mean we should expect to suffer not simply *in* this world but *as* Christians. That's why Peter said,

Beloved, do not be surprised at the fiery trial when it comes

---

3. Dane C. Ortlund, *Deeper: Real Change for Real Sinners* (Wheaton, IL: Crossway, 2021), 128–129.

upon you to test you, as though something strange were happening to you. 13 But rejoice insofar as you share Christ's sufferings, that you may also rejoice and be glad when his glory is revealed. 14 If you are insulted for the name of Christ, you are blessed, because the Spirit of glory and of God rests upon you. (1 Pet. 4:12–14)

Look at this passage. "Suffering," Peter says, "isn't strange. Don't shrink back from it. You should even rejoice!" What? Why? "Because you are sharing in *Christ's* sufferings and by doing so have the *Spirit of truth* rest upon you."

The great lie says suffering is a road to despair; the great truth says suffering is a road to recovery.

Can you see how this response runs completely contrary to the great lie? The great lie, and the great liar, would say, "See! God isn't present with you! He doesn't care about your well being. You're alone. So what if you believe in this Jesus Christ? What does that have to do with your job struggles or your marriage or your food addiction? You're on your own here. Just eak out the rest of your existence as independently as you can. Be the god you want to believe in."

The great lie says suffering is a road to despair; the great truth says suffering is a road to recovery. The great lie says suffering is all about what you want. The great truth says suffering is all about what God is doing. And as Dallas Willard wrote, "Spiritual formation in Christ is the process by which one moves and is moved from self-worship to Christ-centered self-denial as a general condition of life in God's present and eternal kingdom."[4] Let's see if we can paraphrase that with the language we've been using in this book.

> Growing in the great truth of God's presence is the process by which we are moved away from the great lie and towards the divine presence in self-giving, by the power of God's own Spirit, for the glory of God's kingdom.

We are moved to self-giving because of the suffering we face, to offer sympathy and love to those on similar paths, and to push them towards the horizon of eternity. Accepting suffering as a teacher reflects our belief in the great truth: that God *will* restore all things in Christ, and that the Spirit of truth will lead us on the way, through valleys and over mountain peaks. All along the way, the Spirit will work to burn away the great lie that we're all alone, that God isn't with us. In suffering we learn just how *close* God is to us and how deeply he sympathizes with us in our suffering. Sometimes it takes years, maybe even decades, but the Spirit of truth will consume the great lie until there's nothing left but hope and peace.

Turning from a C into a D. Another way we can respond to the Spirit of truth is by turning from a letter C into a letter D.

---

4. Dallas Willard, *Renovation of the Heart: Putting on the Character of Christ*, 10th anniversary ed. (Colorado Springs, CO: NavPress, 2012), 77.

Let me explain what I mean. John Calvin used to say that sin makes us *incurvatus in se,* "curved in on ourselves." We're all like letter Cs. Our necks bend down and in towards our own hearts. We're instinctively self-centered. It takes a work of God to un-curve us. That can also be expressed as a turning away from the great lie—a focus on myself as alone and autonomous—and towards the great truth—that I thrive in relationship with the ever-present God, who calls me to stare at the needs of others. Bending outwards, we start to receive all interactions with a posture of service. It takes some work, but we gaze out past our rounded bellies in order to see others: that's the letter D. In other words, we're always trying to look past ourselves and towards others, whereas letter Cs always look at themselves in spite of others. The Spirit of truth turns us from Cs to Ds. Going down a letter grade, in this case, is a good thing.

The great lie tells us we're on our own, so we might as well look out for number one. In tacitly believing the great lie that God isn't really present, we train our spiritual knecks to bend down and in. We stare at ourselves. The great truth shows us a God who did the very opposite: he stared at us and then gave himself away. *That's* the God we serve, the self-giving truth teller. And the truth is that we only thrive in *relationship* and *dependence* on God, who is always with us.

Turning from a speaker to a listener. Another way we can respond to the Spirit is by holding our tongue. That's much harder than it sounds, partly because we have all sorts of ways in which we only *pretend* to listen. Adam S. McHugh developed an amusing list of these.[5] See if you can identify the common expressions below. We're all guilty here.

- *The one-up.* "You think that's something? Let me tell you about what happened to meet last week!" Here the listener sits quietly through the other person's story only to try to trump them with a better, more interesting story.
- *The sleight of hand.* "Uh huh, that's great. But what I really want to talk to you about is . . ."
- *The inspector.* "Didn't you say last week that . . ." The listener asks as a series of questions . . . trying to lure him into a confession.
- *The reroute.* "That reminds me of . . ."
- *The projector.* "I'm totally dealing with the same thing!" The listener projects his problems onto the speaker, and then projects his solutions onto the speaker's problems.
- *The interrogation.* "What do you think about . . . ? What is your favorite . . . ? Why are you moving to . . . ?" The listener gets wind of the idea that listening is about asking good questions, which is good, but then peppers the speaker with them like a game of dodgeball, which is bad.
- *The password.* "Cheese. I had the best cheese at a dinner party with the mayor last week!" The listener sits quietly through the speaker's conversation, but then seizes on one word that she uses, amid a sea of paragraphs,

5. Adam S. McHugh, *The Listening Life: Embracing Attentiveness in a World of Distraction* (Downers Grove, IL: IVP, 2015), 139–142.

and treats it as a password that unlocks a whole new conversation.

- *The hijack.* [The listener] refrains from speech while the other person talks and then just starts talking about whatever is on his mind.
- *The mechanic.* "Here is what you need to do." This person listens like a mechanic listens to a sputtering engine, trying to diagnose the problem so she can fix it.
- *The bone of contention.* "I disagree with that!" There are an unfortunate number of listeners who listen specifically for what they disagree with.
- *The deflector.* "Yea, but you . . ." This one is a refuge for people who have a hard time receiving criticism, which, let's be honest, is all of us.
- *The boomerang question.* "Did you have a good weekend? Because I . . ." Here a person asks a question of another person with the true intention of answering it herself.

The great lie is actually behind many of our attempts to keep speaking rather than truly listening to others. If God is not really present, then we're all frantically trying to get weight off our chest—in a host of ways: confessing, boasting, envying, complaining, celebrating, reflecting, or maybe just trying to fill the silence with noise because we're uncomfortable. Don't misunderstand, there's nothing wrong with getting things off our chest. We're communicative creatures, after all. But when we do that to the detriment of someone else, we fail as listeners. The great lie suggests no God is here to listen to our souls in secret. When we believe that, even quietly, we start pouring out words to others in a frenzy, because we want *someone* to hear us.

The Spirit of truth tells us that God is always listening, always hearing. It's part of his nature. "In God's very being, communication does not move unilaterally but flows back and forth and around the three persons of the Trinity—Father, Son, and Holy Spirit. The triune nature of God puts listening right at the center of the universe. God is love, and love requires listening."[6] While we discussed the Word as God's answer to the great lie, which highlights God's truthful speech, it's also true that the Spirit of truth is always listening. Jesus said, "when the Spirit of truth comes, he will guide you into all the truth, for he will not speak on his own authority, but whatever he *hears* he will speak" (John 16:13; emphasis added). The Spirit of truth always hears. He always listens. When we receive the Word of truth, Jesus Christ, we also receive the Spirit, and that means we receive an eternal *listener*. Becoming more like the Spirit, then, means growing in our ability to listen to others. This is a tangible way to discern if and how we're responding to the Spirit.

We forget that there's a road to walk in Christ-conformity, and you go down a road by taking one step at a time, not by jumping a mile every moment.

---

6. McHugh, *The Listening Life*, 36.

Finding beauty in development. Another way we can respond to the Spirit of truth is by recognizing and accepting something *very* difficult for us in contemporary western culture: we're all in process. We're all still developing in our maturity and Christ-likeness. In fact, there's *beauty* in that development. We're very quick to focus on "results" and even perfection. We forget that there's a *road* to walk in Christ-conformity, and you go down a road by taking one step at a time, not by jumping a mile every moment. John Murray wrote of this in a way that's always stuck with me. Look at what he says.

> The child who acts as a man is a monstrosity; the man who acts as a child is a tragedy. If this is true in nature, how much more in Christian behavior. There are babes in Christ; there are young men, and there are old men. And what monstrosities and tragedies have marred the witness of the church by failure to take account of the law of growth![7]

Murray is saying we ignore the fact that we're all in process, in development, at various stages of growth in Christ. But guess what? God has *ordained* this. He could have declared that we'd all become immediately like Christ when we professed belief in him, but he didn't. And what God does is true and good and beautiful. Isn't it hard for us to accept this? Don't we all long for immediate change? And don't we find slow progress repulsive? But God *doesn't*.

---

7. John Murray, *Collected Writings of John Murray* (Carlisle, PA: Banner of Truth, 1977), 2:298–99.

The great lie, again, is behind some of this. If God isn't really here with us, then we're all in control of our own development, and the faster it happens, the better. If we're not maturing quickly, it reflects badly on us; it embarrasses us. We feel ashamed. Granted, some shame may play a positive role in our growth. But do you ever pause to reflect on how far you've come? This is one of the reasons why I'm an advocate of people keeping a journal. It lets you see the past, and how different you were back then, how much more you've become like the Word of truth. We tend to ignore the past instantaneously and stare at the future ravenously. We want more, we want it faster, and we want it in perfection.

Living in the Spirit of truth and trusting in God's presence means we submit to his plan for us, which apparently includes some slow growth over long periods of time. Think of yourself spiritually as a toddler first learning to speak. My son used to have various substitutions for words he couldn't say yet.

- Mnamna – tomato
- Boomba – ball
- Klucalah – clementine

Over months, those words would be replaced by the next stage of development.

- Mato
- Ba
- Clem

Eventually, the full forms would come in. And every parent will know what I mean when I say this: *That was actually a bit sad*. We were going to miss all those toddler appropriations of English. Why? Because development is beautiful. Growth is beautiful—not just the end result but the *process*. When the process is beautiful, then each step is beautiful. Trusting in the Spirit of truth means trusting in the God who redeems us through process. Development is beautiful.

Learning to let go. I left this until last because it's the most threatening for us. The ultimate trust in the Spirit of truth is trust that life conquers death. The older you get, the more often you see those you love walking into the silent country. Death takes and takes and takes. But it can't really take you. In a previous chapter, I talked about staring at eternity in the face of death and claiming the truth of our own immortality in Christ. Here, I'm focused more on the decision to let go of earthly things so that we can stare more longingly at heavenly ones.

Once again, the great lie comes to tear us down. The great lie says that if we can't feel God's presence on earth, what confidence should we have in his promises to care for us in and after death? If we're all on our own here, then we're all on our own there.

But the Spirit of truth calls for trust. All of us, in the end, will have to look at the impenetrable curtain of death and say, "God, I trust you." I say this as someone who thinks about death all too often. My favorite lines from Henry Wadsworth Longfellow always comfort me here, and they resonate with the great truth of Christ's conquering of death.

Life is real! Life is earnest!
    And the grave is not its goal;
Dust thou art, to dust returnest,
    Was not spoken of the soul.

Living in the Spirit of truth is our response to the Word of truth. There are many different responses. We've only explored some of them in this chapter. The important thing is that we're responding to the Word of truth in some way, and that we're *intentional* about it. Dallas Willard reminds us,

> Projects of personal transformation rarely if ever succeed by accident, drift, or imposition. Indeed, where accident, drift, and imposition dominate—as they usually do, quite frankly, in the lives of professing Christians—very little of any human value transpires. Effective action has to involve order, subordination, and progression, developing from the inside of the personality.[1]

There's a lot in that quote to unpack. But what he's saying about "order, subordination, and progression" has to do with *intentionality*, with our having made a *decision* to trace our response to the Spirit of truth, who applies the Word of truth to our hearts. Many of us have a hard time being intentional about our response to the Word of truth, but without that,

---

1. Willard, *Renovation of the Heart*, 83.

we're prone to fall into the great lie again, to act as if God weren't present and working in the details of our lives. Even choosing one way each day, after reading God's Word, and looking at how the Spirit of truth is working on our hearts in that area can make a big difference. And it can push us on to keep responding to the presence of God in our lives each day.

Reflection Questions and Prayer

1. Can you explain to someone else how the Spirit of truth is related to the Word of truth in our spiritual development?
2. How does the Spirit of truth work to combat the great lie in one particular area for you?
3. Aside from those listed in this chapter, what other ways can we respond to the Spirit of truth? You can think of both positive and negative ways.

Prayer

Spirit of the living God,
Applier of the great Word of truth,
Dwell richly in me.
Help me trace you working,
And draw my heart away
From every lie of Satan.
Show me how his great lie
Is false. Again. And again. And again.
Make me more like the Word of truth

So that the world might know
That you have sent yourself to us,
That you have spoken truth
Where falsehood reigned.

12

CONCLUSION: STEEPING IN GOD'S PRESENCE

I n many ways, this book has been a call to steep in the presence of God, to rid ourselves of the great lie and cling to the Word of truth, the one who promises to be with us always. God still grants us his spoken presence (creation speech and special speech). Yet, since we have accepted the Word of truth, God's response to the great lie, the Spirit of truth now dwells inside us. God is more than just *present*; he's present *inside* us.

But I know that when you put this book down, life will go on as usual. You and I will still face daily threats from the great lie. We'll have days when we feel as if God is absent. But we'll also have days where we have the opportunity to steep in God's presence, to draw all of our attention there in the power of the Spirit. What does that look like? I'm ending the book with an example, which I hope will set you on your own path. Daily meditating on the great truth of God's presence with you can truly set you free from every spiritual plight that follows from the great lie. It can sure up your faith and your hope in an eternal life with the God of truth. And that, in turn, will help you see the rest of your life in perspective. The truth of God's presence will lead us ahead, and it will lead us home.

What follows is just one example of how I like to "steep" in God's presence, soaking up his presence into the fibers of my soul.

Steeping in the Presence of God

Two amber lights glow in the early morning dark that hovers around our family room. The light seems to whisper to the corners and angles of the window trim, accenting the detail before the wild sun covers it over for the day. Children's books sleep slanted on a bottom shelf, resting on a basket as a boulder. The two potted plants on the top shelf are silent, but still growing, still living. They soak in tiny amounts of water through their sleeping tertiary roots and release vapor into the air through the stomata on the undersides of their leaves. I don't hear any of this happening. I don't see it, either. But it's happening. God is *here*—behind the vapor and the photons and the shadows. Beyond the senses, he is here . . . *speaking himself*.

There's a gold and black globe resting on the top of a hutch that belonged to my wife's grandparents. From where I sit in the corner of the room, the light is moving just over South America. What's happening there, on that other continent, right now? I have absolutely no idea. But God is *there*. He spoke everything I see and don't see into existence, and in that speech, in the simple making, he is present. His creation whispers it, in some mysterious tongue of *telos*, of purpose—the lights and the books and the basket, the black globe and the old hutch. Everything I see might as well nod and say, "Mmmhmm. His eternal power and divine nature . . . Do you get it?"

Sometimes I want to say out loud, "No, I don't." But the grace and patience of God tells me that *my* perception isn't the thing at stake here. The *truth* is at stake, the personhood of God present in the room, and that truth, flowering in the great Word of truth, is thick and strong as mountain roots. God always waits for me to catch up, like a father ten feet ahead of his toddler on the beach. I'll get there. And he'll stay until I do. And even if I don't get there, he'll stay. He can't do otherwise than be who he is, than be everywhere.

I need to take the truth of God's presence, the bedrock notion that he's here, right now, and sit on it. This is where I need to rest. But it's more than that. It's not just a platitude, an idea I touch down on when I feel curious or awed or unsettled. No—I don't think I need to sit on it; I think I need to *steep* in it, like crushed tea leaves in boiling water, letting out their scent and flavor in the water's embrace. I need to be tea leaves. I need to steep my soul in the Spirit of truth, letting it infiltrate every pore and crevice.

That all sounds good and poetic, but what does it really mean? It means I need to walk into a room and greet him first, because he was there before I was. As we've seen, God is so great and spiritually broad-backed, and we're so blinded by the great lie, that we *really* think we're the first one in the room. We never are. Say it again, and let it sink in. *I'm never the first one in the room.* I'm never the first one in my office, the first one in a field, the first one on the edge of the garden, where the white peonies are bowing their heavy heads in worship. I'm never the first. Never.

Steeping in the presence of God in this way means that I let the truth not simply *confront* me but *affect* me. I let myself respond to the Spirit of truth. When something confronts us, like a stranger on the street, it puts itself in our path. We have to acknowledge it, give an awkward greeting, at least. But when something affects us, it gets under our skin. It swims in our blood. It changes how we meet the world. We have to respond somehow.

I love Annie Dillard's prose. It's meditative, sharply observant, and spiritually alert. In her Pulitzer prize winning *Pilgrim at Tinker Creek*, she observes many things in the wild world around her. These observations shape and invigorate her. Look at how she describes watching muskrats, for instance. Look at how this affects her.

It was late dusk; I was driving home from a visit with friends. Just on the off chance I parked quietly by the creek, walked out on the narrow bridge over the shallows, and looked upstream. Someday, I had been telling myself for weeks, someday a muskrat is going to swim right through that channel in the cattails, and I am going to see it. That is precisely what happened. I looked up into the channel for a muskrat, and there it came, swimming right toward me. Knock; seek; ask. It seemed to swim with a side-to-side, sculling motion of its vertically flattened tail. It looked bigger than the upside-down muskrat, and its face more reddish. In its mouth it clasped a twig of tulip tree. One thing amazed me: it swam right down the middle of the creek. I thought it would hide in the brush along the edge; instead, it plied the waters as obviously as an aquaplane. I could just look and look.

But I was standing on the bridge, not sitting, and it saw me. It changed its course, veered towards the bank, and disappeared behind an indentation in the rushy shoreline. I felt a rush of such pure energy. I thought I would not need to breathe for days.[2]

I want to steep in God's presence the way Annie Dillard watches muskrats. I want God's presence to change me, to make me feel as if simply being aware of him seems more precious than breathing. I want God's presence to *affect* me. Don't you?

Now, steeping in the truth is very different from sensing the truth as an idea. We're good at the latter but not so skilled with the former. We rush. We hurry. And hurry is a form of violence on the soul.[3]

Do a little experiment with me as we end this conversation together. Read through the following descriptions of God's omnipresence. How do they strike you?

- Infinity in the sense of not being confined by space is synonymous with God's omnipresence. This attribute too is most vividly represented in Scripture. God is the creator, and all that exists is and remains his in an absolute sense. He is the Lord, the possessor of heaven

---

2. Annie Dillard, *Pilgrim at Tinker Creek* (New York: Harper Perennial Modern Classics, 1998), 194.

3. John Mark Comer, *The Ruthless Elimination of Hurry: How to Stay Emotionally Healthy and Spiritually Alive in the Chaos of the Modern World* (Colorado Springs, CO: Waterbook, 2019), 47.

and earth (Gen. 14:19, 22; Deut. 10:14), exalted above all creatures, also above all space. Heaven and earth cannot contain him, how much less an earthly temple (1 Kings 8:27; 2 Chron. 2:6; Isa. 66:1; Acts 7:48), but neither is he excluded from space. He fills heaven and earth [with his presence]. No one can hide from him. He is a God at hand no less than a God from afar (Jer. 23:23, 24; Ps. 139:7–10; Acts 17:27).[4]

- We . . . begin with the internal fulness of the being of God as the positive foundation for the created world and, therefore, of its spatial aspect. It is this self-existent being who has created the world by an act of his will, and who can and must therefore be present to all space with the fulness of his being in order that it may exist at all.[5]

- [God's] ability to manifest himself to people in any place stands upon his actual presence in all places. God's immensity (literally, "no measure") means that he cannot be confined to any one place or limited by any boundary. . . . God's *immensity* means that he is the Lord of space. Geerhardus Vos said, "He is exalted above all distinction of space, yet at every point in space is present with all His being and as such is the cause of space." Athanasius said, "God is self-existent, enclosing all things, and enclosed by none." As the self-existent One, God is his own home,

---

4. Herman Bavinck, *Reformed Dogmatics*, vol. 2, *God and Creation*, ed. John Bolt, trans. John Vriend (Grand Rapids, MI: Baker Academic, 2004), 164.

5. Cornelius Van Til, *An Introduction to Systematic Theology: Prolegomena and the Doctrines of Revelation, Scripture, and God*, 2n ed., ed. William Edgar (Phillipsburg, NJ: P&R, 2007), 340.

so to speak. Augustine wrote, "Before God made heaven and earth, before he made the saints, where did he dwell? He dwelt in himself." God's immensity, however, does not locate him outside of space, as if he were absent from his creation, but implies that he is present throughout creation.[6]

How do you respond? With an "amen"? With a head-nod? *That's not good enough.*

Please understand, I'm not trying to be harsh. I'm just thinking of the muskrats. These theologians I've quoted are brothers whom I love and respect. They've taught me much. And yet it's not enough to give a head-nod to God's omnipresence. It needs to *affect* us, not just *confront* us.

How do we do this? How do we respond to God's presence? We've looked at some ways in the previous chapter. But I'll leave you with just one concrete approach, one that's come up again and again in our discussion. To make something concrete, you have to see it incarnate in your surroundings. It's not enough for God to be present in an Italian countryside (unless you happen to be living in the Italian countryside right now). He has to be present in your kitchen, near that spot by the oven where grape jelly clings to the grain of the wood floor.

Always in the Room

On a practical level, I think of this as the simple truth I've often

6. Joel R. Beeke and Paul M. Smalley, *Reformed Systematic Theology*, vol. 1, *Revelation and God* (Wheaton, IL: Crossway, 2019), 651–652.

repeated: *God is always in the room.* Conceptually, we know this is true, but we seldom think about it, let alone have it influence our behavior. In the terms used earlier, we receive the Word of truth, but we haven't let the Spirit of the truth apply it. But consider what happens when we do.

It's 4:00am. The hum of my daughter's sound machine fills the air with white noise. My eyes are open, blinking in the dark as I stare at the silhouettes of unicorns and computer-paper crayon drawings on the wall. In our family, sleep has been a game of musical chairs lately. Our youngest moves to mom and dad's bed; dad moves into her bed to keep the other one company. It's not so common for me to wake up where I actually went to sleep. In this stage of life, I'm a nightly nomad.

As I stare at the walls, I'm thinking of my father's little sister, who just found out she has cancer. Her brother, my dad, passed from cancer in 2004. My life's definition for the word *shatter* is watching him die in front of me on that surreal night in June. My godfather, a seasoned Christian counselor and my father's best friend, says that my anxiety disorder (nearly fifteen years old and still going strong) may well have been a PTSD response to that very night. Learning of my aunt's cancer is bringing up baggage I thought I'd dealt with already. But we're never really finished dealing with things in the way we imagine, are we?

As I'm praying for her—that the peace of God would wash over her and renew her spirit in the face of mortality—I'm realizing that my fear of death, of ending, isn't dead yet. I'd ignored it long enough to imagine it was gone and buried. And here it was, dancing in the dark of my daughter's room as I tried (unsuccessfully) to go back to sleep.

And then it dawned on me that God wasn't just able to see my thoughts from afar (Ps. 139:2), to watch the swirling chaos of ambition, hope, love, passion, fear, and envy break through my consciousness a few days before Halloween in 2021; he was also here. He was in the room, just as he's in the room right now as I write this. I can't see him. I can only see the shadows and lines of light marking the wall as the dazing applause of the sound machine drifts down the hallway. The great lie is always hovering over my spirit like a cloud, enticing me in shadows to believe that God *isn't* really here, that it's just me wandering through my own insecurities and fears of death, rummaging through a thousand memories of my dad and my aunt, staring at the strange truth that things don't go on forever, that there is something called an *end*.

I identify the lie more easily these days, which I like to think ticks the devil off. (I'm happy to tick off the one partially responsible for bringing cancer into this world.) And so I start to pray, assuming that God really is here, in *this* room.

> God, please give my aunt peace and courage that transcends her.
> Fill her with a light of hope that refuses to go out.
> May the pain of this lead her ever deeper into your love,
> Ever deeper into the beauty of how all of life is a gift,
> And that gift gets unwrapped moment by moment.
> Help me, as well, as I confront once more the fear of death.
> I can feel the devil discouraging me with disbelief.

He is a liar. He wants me to be hopeless.

By your Spirit, I will *never* be hopeless.

Father, keep conforming me to your Son,

Especially in faith, since that's what I long for

But never seem to grasp for very long.

I know you will be faithful.

I know that *death* is not for me because *you* are for me.

Nothing will ever separate me from you. Nothing.

Now, make me a light to my family this day. Amen.

I get up before my alarm goes off. I'm familiar enough with my own body to know when it's pointless to try to go back to sleep. I wander out to the kitchen to make coffee, and then I sit down to keep writing this chapter, the one you hold in your hands.

If the truth is anything, it's a rock. Rock doesn't bend to you; *you bend to* it.

The truth that *God is always in the room* isn't always as mystical as it sounds. Sometimes it's just a refrain we sing silently, something we set our souls on, refusing to give in to the great lie that plays to our post-Enlightenment doubt of everything supernatural. If the truth is anything, it's a rock (Isa. 26:4). Rock doesn't bend to *you*; you bend to *it*. My doubts and fears met the granite of God that night. My unbelieving thoughts eventually fell away. I remembered again who I am in God. I am a creature in God's spoken world, born to speak with him, equipped by God's own Spirit to assault every lie of the devil with Jesus's clarion call to believe (John 20:27). God is here.

What It Means to Steep

Steeping in God's presence means both affirming the truth of God's *here-ness* and then speaking to him where you are. It's that simple: *affirm* and *speak*. If you can't do that, then your spongy heart hasn't absorbed what those theologians I quoted earlier referred to as God's omnipresence. Your head may have absorbed it, but your heart hasn't. Remember that there's a difference between *knowing* what something means and *believing* that it's true. Belief means taking action to become the person God made you to be in Christ Jesus. Many of us know about God's omnipresence, but we don't really believe that it's true. We don't act on it at 4:00am when we're trying to fall back asleep. But that's *precisely* when believing is most critical. Belief hardly ever blossoms in a quiet garden by itself. Its petals push out in praise right when the rest of the weeds are trying to pull it down or steal the water from its roots.

To switch metaphors, belief happens in the dark. It doesn't *borrow* light from the room; it *makes* its own light, since it comes from God, and God *is* light (1 John 1:5). To steep in God's presence is to return—morning after morning, afternoon by afternoon, night after night—to the great truth that God is always in the room. He's always with you, even *in* you.

May this day and the rest of your days be a testament to that truth. It's time to rid ourselves daily of the great lie, and to live in light of the great truth.

Reflection Questions and Prayer

1. Describe a moment when you felt you were *steeping* in God's presence.
2. What's the difference between *acknowledging* a doctrine such as God's omnipresence and *embracing* it as true in your own life?
3. How does the truth that *God is always in the room* help you spiritually?
4. What sorts of experiences seem to shout the great lie at you? What's a passage of Scripture you can memorize and recite during those moments? Remember what you have learned about receiving the Word of truth and then responding to the Spirit of truth.

Prayer

God, I know about the doctrine of omnipresence.
It's a beautiful . . . *idea.*
But I know my heart is slow to believe it,
To embrace it as *truth.*
Spirit, help me in my unbelief.
Help me to affirm your presence with me everywhere
And to speak back to you in faith.
Help me to spot the Great Lie
Wherever it creeps into my daily life.
Make me ready to drive it away with faith.

FEEDBACK

I want to hear from you! Was this book helpful? Did it provide what you were hoping you'd find? Would you recommend it to a friend? The best way you can express your thoughts on the book and let others know about it is to leave a review on Amazon or Goodreads. This helps other strugglers get a sense of what they can expect from the book. It's also a huge help to writers! Would you do that for me? Just follow the instructions below for Amazon. It's similar for Goodreads.

- Go to my Amazon author page (amazon.com/author/piercetaylorhibbs) and click on this book.
- Click next to the Amazon rating, which will show you the current reviews.
- Click the button that says "Write a customer review."
- Follow the steps to leave your review.

I'm legitimately interested in what you think. Be honest. I promise I won't be offended. Thank you for reading the book! That in itself is a huge blessing to me.

Connect and Grow

Want to connect with me and grow in your spiritual development? You can join my email list to get free downloads that will help, and maybe you'll pick up some inspiration on the way. I'll keep you posted about new publications and give you exclusive content, too! There aren't any strings attached.

To join, visit https://piercetaylorhibbs.substack.com and subscribe to my newsletter. Hope to see you there!

Ingram Content Group UK Ltd.
Milton Keynes UK
UKHW012153200323
418875UK00003B/95

9 798986 106717